*Anne Carminati* | J



# 111 Museums in Paris That You Shouldn't Miss

111

emons:

To my two daughters Olivia and Julianne,
the loves of my life and my true inspiration.
*Anne Carminati*

To Michèle Marchadier, without whom
my Parisian adventures would never have been possible.
*James Wesolowski*

MIX
Paper from responsible sources
FSC® C043106


Layout: Eva Kraskes, based on a design
by Lübbeke | Naumann | Thoben
Maps: altancicek.design, www.altancicek.de
Basic cartographical information from Openstreetmap,
© OpenStreetMap-Mitwirkende, OdbL
Editing: Karen E. Seiger
Printing and binding: Grafisches Centrum Cuno, Calbe
Printed in Germany 2024
First edition 2023
ISBN 978-3-7408-2363-4
Revised second edition, May 2024

Guidebooks for Locals & Experienced Travelers
Join us in uncovering new places around the world at
www.111places.com

# Foreword

We joined forces to write this guide to the museums of Paris from two different perspectives. Anne, a native Frenchwoman, developed her artistic eye through drawing, painting, and exploring museums. She lived in New York for 20 years before returning to Paris. James, an American technologist, loves both New York, where he also lived for 20 years, and Paris, which he now considers home. We approached this guidebook in a way that best suited our individual interests and knowledge. Anne focused on the venerable fine art institutions, and James visited the small, the curious, and the off-the-beaten path museums. This book is the proud result of our collaboration.

Among native Parisians, it is fashionable to visit all the latest temporary exhibitions so as to engage in lively, informed conversations. Indeed, one of the most interesting aspects of the Paris Metro is the number of posters advertising museum exhibitions – you can schedule your cultural activities during your commute. For visitors, the grand tour of Paris always includes the Louvre and the Orsay Museum, or the Paris Catacombs. This guide conveys a different message to each group.

To our fellow Parisians, we urge you to visit the museums' permanent collections, particularly if you have not seen them since childhood. They are filled with treasures and stories that will rekindle your sense of discovery. These collections represent a unique heritage that belongs to Paris and France alone. Take advantage of the immense care, passion, and attention to detail that go into each and every museum.

To visitors, do visit the big institutions, as they are wonderful. But to profit fully from all that Paris has to offer, seek out the smaller museums too. Learn about history that is not your own, and explore culture and innovation from a uniquely French perspective. You'll find something to amaze you in every arrondissement.

# 111 Museums

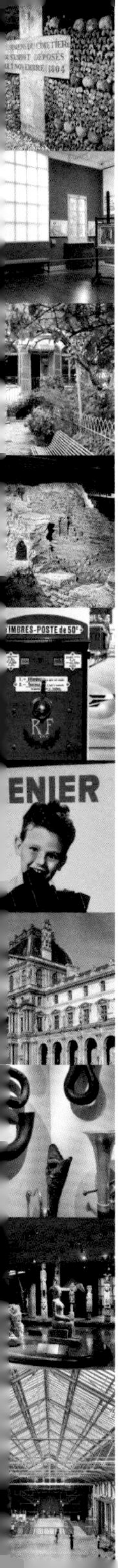

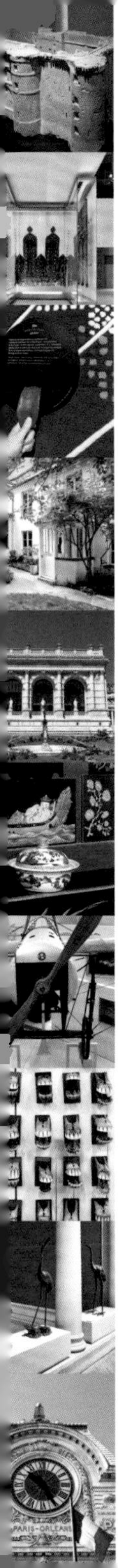

# 1 Air and Space Museum

*France's proud history of flight*

Le Bourget is the perfect place for a museum dedicated to flight. As France's first commercial airport, Le Bourget serves as a powerful reminder of the nation's vital contribution to aviation. As you arrive at the historic airport, you'll be struck by the beauty of its art deco architecture, and then you'll embark on a journey through several eras of flight.

The Pioneers of the Air Hall in the original terminal building makes this museum truly special. France jumpstarted aviation with hot-air balloons and dirigibles. Balloon baskets and nacelles, art and scientific artifacts, graphic posters, and even a balloon-themed bidet pay testimony to an early fascination with flight.

French plane designers and airmen were also pioneers in the years leading up to World War I, and the museum is full of fanciful but airworthy designs. Imagine taking to the skies in the 1906 Trajan Vuia "airplane-car" or the delicate 1908 Demoiselle designed by Alberto Santos-Dumont. Competitions spurred development of new airplanes and the emergence of new French heroes. The museum houses a Blériot Type XI-2, a two-seat version of the plane that Louis Blériot used to cross the English Channel in 1909, as well as the Morane-Saulnier G used by Roland Garros to cross the Mediterranean from France to Tunisia in 1913.

Other memorable designs of the period include the 1908 Antoinette Type VII, which resembles a rowboat with wings and a huge engine strapped to its front; the 1912 Farman HF.20, a flying washtub and the first plane designed specifically for military use; and the bird-like 1910 Fabre Hydravion, the world's first seaplane.

The Air and Space Museum includes its share of more recent airplanes and spaceships too. There are extensive collections of military planes, two Concordes, and Ariane 1 and 5 rockets. You can walk through a Boeing 747 and get up close to a double-decker Airbus A380.

Address 3 esplanade de l'Air et de l'Espace, 93352 Le Bourget, +33 (0)1 49 92 70 62, www.museeairespace.fr | Getting there Bus 152 to Le Bourget | Hours See website for seasonal hours | Tip Among the thousands of memorial plaques across Paris, the one at 299 boulevard Saint-Germain in the 7th arrondissement marks the last residence of Louis Blériot.

# 2 Antique Lighting Museum

*Explore the beauty of lamplight*

Some of the most compelling museums represent the expertise of passionate and knowledgeable private collectors. Certainly, owner Ara Kebapcioglu and his Antique Lighting Museum is a prime example. Housed in a diminutive storefront in the 5th arrondissement, the museum is filled floor-to-ceiling with desk, wall, and ceiling lamps, and it doubles as a showroom for collectors, decorators, and others interested in the unique and spectacular lamps designed in the age of kerosene, petrol, and oil.

The collection's several hundred lamps serve as both décor and history lesson and illustrate the continuous advancements in lighting between the late 18th century and the start of the 20th century, and the ascendance of incandescent light. The lamps come in myriad styles that are decorative, whimsical, and practical. They reflect different needs and tastes, the type of light that was required from each lamp, and the available technology.

Call ahead to request a one-on-one tour of this fascinating collection. Mr. Kebapcioglu, a polyglot, world traveler, and all-around bon vivant, is an encyclopedia into the world of lighting. He will be happy to demonstrate the workings of several lamps and to assemble and light up a few of his favorites, such as the Quinquet-type oil lamp from Ramier, an earthenware petrol lamp with an ornate lampshade from Nouvelle Imagerie d'Epinal, or an early art nouveau filament bulb.

The process of lighting and maintaining an oil or gas lamp is fascinating to those who have only ever seen them in pictures and movies, and the resulting glow of the light within its housing is positively entrancing.

In recognition of the historical importance of the collection, the museum recently donated several lamps to the Musée Carnavalet. But anyone compelled by their beauty and luminosity is welcome to purchase and take home one of these unique objects.

**Address** 4 rue Flatters, 75005 Paris, +33 (0)1 47 07 63 47, www.lumieredeloeil.com, Lumiara@aol.com | **Getting there** Metro to Les Gobelins (Line 7); bus 21, 83, 91 to Port Royal-Berthollet | **Hours** By appointment only | **Tip** Paris and its suburbs were at one time lit by gas streetlamps, and you can find the last working one, known as Léon, on the Sentier du Tir in Malakoff near the Porte de Vanves.

# 3 Arab World Institute

*A bridge between two cultures*

A prime location, award-winning architecture, fascinating temporary exhibitions, and a fantastic bookstore. The Arab World Institute has everything that makes for a spectacular museum. Originally intended as a bridge between France and the Middle East, it has become a center of learning about Arab history and culture. While Islam is central to understanding the modern Arab world, the museum explores an Arab culture that dates to East-West trade routes established around 1000 B.C. Religion is but one theme here, encompassing three major world faiths with origins in the region.

The collection is divided into areas that address several themes, including the early Arab world, family life, math and science, and art and beauty. Panels provide detailed explanations of Arabic terms and traditions, which are brought to life with an incredible set of historic artifacts.

A great example of the museum's design is the exhibit on family life. The panel explains that the typical urban house consists of public and private spaces often separated by an open-air atrium and fountain. So the museum has recreated these spaces with two display alcoves and an ornately tiled fountain between them. If you face the alcove for the private inner space, a brilliantly colored rectangular textile, or *izar*, hangs where you would find the doorway, providing both airflow and privacy.

The museum also makes innovative use of sound. As you approach an area with objects from different religious structures, speakers in the ceiling play a mosque's call to prayer, while songs echo through a sacred church space. Almost imperceptible at first, you soon realize how effectively sound is used to add another rich layer to the exhibits. In the hammam, you'll hear conversation and laughter against the sound of running water. And among a display of musical instruments, you'll hear the strains of an oud.

Address 1 rue des Fossés-Saint-Bernard, Place Mohammed-V, 75005 Paris, +33 (0)1 40 51 38 38, www.imarabe.org | Getting there Metro to Jussieu (Lines 7, 10); bus 67, 75, 87, 90 to Institut du Monde Arabe | Hours Tue–Fri 10am–6pm, Sat & Sun 10am–7pm | Tip The back wall of the Institute facing Quai Saint-Bernard and the Biology Research Library features an incredible mural by the Tunisian French artist eL Seed (www.elseed-art.com).

# 4 Archeological Crypt

*Return to Lutèce*

Millions of tourists pass through the square in front of Notre Dame on the way to the cathedral, the Île Saint-Louis, or the Left or Right Banks. It's a historic and picturesque walk. But look for the small stairway near the street labeled "Crypte Archeologique." Therein lie the true origins of the city of Paris.

Well before the current city was renamed Paris and the great cathedral was built, the Île de la Cité was a settlement of the Gallic Parisii people and later the center of the 4th-century Roman city of Lutèce. When Germanic tribes started to invade Gaul, the settlements on the Left Bank near rue Soufflot and boulevard Saint-Michel were abandoned, and the stones of the forum were used to construct a rampart on the island. Flash forward to Paris in 1965. There are now parking spaces in front of Notre Dame, and plans are underway to create an underground car park. Digging revealed part of the Roman city extending underneath most of the area of the square. The current museum was opened in 1980, and it consists of a large area of excavated remains of early structures surrounded by a viewing walkway and temporary exhibits. The ruins themselves reveal the history of the city starting with 4th-century fortifications and the changing cold and hot rooms of the Roman baths. Walls outline rooms, curved archways mark the entrances to buildings, and column fragments remain. Although the major archeological work occurred in the years following the crypt's discovery, artifacts such as Lutetian coins are still being found.

The crypt also reveals how cities expand, particularly along their riverbanks. The oldest part of the ruins includes the walls and steps down to the 1st-century Roman wharf along the Seine. You can imagine a boat tied up alongside the wharf to deliver wheat to the city. Nineteen centuries later, the wharf is 55 meters (180 feet) from the river's edge.

Address 7 place Jean II, 75004 Paris, +33 (0)1 55 42 50 10, www.crypte.paris.fr, carnavalet.actionculturelle@paris.fr | Getting there Metro to Saint Michel (Line 4); RER B, C to Saint Michel-Notre Dame; bus 47, 75 to Cité-Parvis Notre-Dame | Hours Tue–Sun 10am–6pm | Tip A substantial piece of the early Roman city on the Left Bank exists to this day at the Arènes de Lutèce, now in the midst of a busy park (49 rue Monge).

# 5 Army Health Service Museum

*Tragic advances in medical science*

The former abbey of Val-de-Grâce was supported by Queen Anne d'Autriche, who added a spectacular church to celebrate the birth of Louis XIV. You can see the church, with its baldaquin resembling Saint Peter's in Rome and the cupola fresco by Pierre Mignard, as part of your visit to the Army Heath Service Museum. As with many museums in Paris, the building's architecture adds to its allure.

Don't miss the collection of Dr. François Debat. Among the historical mortars, vessels and pitchers, travel kits, and microscopes are some fine examples of 16th to 18th-century Italian faience.

Upstairs, the museum highlights the history of the service and the role that war plays in the development of new and improved medical practices. This was particularly true of World War I, during which the service was forced to address an unprecedented scale of injuries. The museum features an extensive exhibit on evacuation, including a variety of stretchers used to get the injured off the front lines. New types of vehicles, including motorized ambulances, hospital trains, and airplanes, transported soldiers to more extensive care. Mobile radiological suites were introduced, thanks to the efforts of Marie Curie.

Nerve gas inflicted mass casualties, and a display shows several models of masks used by French forces. Infantry charges created horrific head injuries, and wax models illustrate improvements to maxillo-facial surgery. A final display of patients, doubled over and limbs stuck in unnatural positions, represents the many ways in which shell shock would manifest physically in its victims.

The last and more hopeful exhibit focuses on the service's efforts to eradicate viral diseases, control parasitic infections like malaria, and improve individual and collective hygiene. Disease can harm an army and a population as badly as bullets and bombs.

Address 1 place Alphonse Laveran, 75005 Paris, +33 (0)1 40 51 51 92, evdg.sante.defense.gouv.fr/le-musee/decouvrir-le-musee, ssa-musee.contact.fct@def.gouv.fr | Getting there RER B to Port-Royal; bus 83, 91 to Port Royal-Saint-Jacques | Hours Tue–Sun 11am–6pm | Tip The 18th-century Hôtel de Massa was relocated in 1929 from the Champs Elysees to the nearby gardens of the Paris Observatory (38 rue du Faubourg Saint-Jacques, www.sgdl.org).

# 6__Army Museum

*Military history and bizarre musical instruments*

Les Invalides pays tribute to France's impressive military history. Originally a hospital for soldiers of the Napoleonic wars, the compound, with its distinct gilded cupola, now displays hundreds of years of military uniforms, weaponry, and equipment. Interactive and narrated dioramas depict how battles were won and lost. The dangers of battle are nowhere more dramatically displayed than through a breastplate that has been neatly and devastatingly pierced by a cannon ball during the Battle of Waterloo.

As you might imagine, General Napoleon is well represented in the museum. As the timeline crosses into the 19th century, you will find many artifacts emblematic of his reign, as well as the magnificent portrait by Jean-Auguste-Dominique Ingres. Le Vizir, his last horse from his exile on Elba, stands stuffed nearby. The adjoining Church of the Dome holds Napoleon's famous tomb and memorial.

In the midst of all the history and pageantry, however, is a small exhibit that must not be overlooked. Groups of musical instruments from French military bands are displayed in a small room labeled "Extra Ordinary Cabinets." Some of the instruments are easily recognizable, but you'll encounter many more that look only vaguely familiar. Brass instruments that appear to be trumpets or French horns have way too many valves.

Several versions of bassoon appear unlike anything in a modern orchestra. A trombone has a large mouth like a mythological beast. Brass instruments called "serpents" that were used in the church and in the military share the graceful curves of their namesakes. The obvious question is, "What sounds do they make?" Simply press a numbered button on the reference panels in front of the displays for a recording of the associated instrument. You will hear for yourself why they made a six-valve trombone, and that this serpent does not actually hiss.

**Address** Hôtel National des Invalides, 129 rue de Grenelle, 75007 Paris, +33 (0)1 44 42 38 77, www.musee-armee.fr | **Getting there** Metro to La Tour-Marbourg (Line 8), Saint François-Xavier (Line 13), Varenne (Line 13); RER C to Invalides; bus 28 to Invalides-La Tour Marbourg, 69 to Esplanade des Invalides, 89, 92 to Vauban-Hôtel des Invalides | **Hours** Daily 10am–6pm | **Tip** To see all the museums of Paris, you're going to need a good pair of walking shoes. Visit Magfred Chaussures on the pedestrian street of Rue Cler for comfortable, French-made shoes from Mephisto (49 rue Cler, www.magfred.com).

# 7 Arts and Industry Museum

*Echoes of the past*

The Room of Echoes in the Arts and Industry Museum has a close association with the former priory of Saint-Martin-des-Champs and a curious connection to Grand Central Terminal in New York City.

Like the vestibule outside the entrance to the Oyster Bar in Grand Central, the Room of Echoes has an arched ceiling. So one person can face the wall in one corner of the room and another person at the diagonally opposite corner can hear whatever they are saying. Unlike Grand Central, the acoustics in the Room of Echoes have a purpose tied to its former life as part of the accompanying church. In its early years, the room served as a confessional for lepers, who could recount their sins to a priest stationed at the opposite corner in an early form of social distancing.

The Fardier de Cugnot sits in the same space and is a fascinating and enormous example of early engineering for which the museum is justly famous. Built in 1769, over a hundred years before the first internal combustion engine, it was a large, three-wheeled cart that was designed to be a military vehicle for carrying heavy loads, such as artillery. The huge water tank at the front drove a steam engine that propelled it forward. At 4 kph (2.5 mph), it was not very fast, nor was it easy to turn, but it is still amazing to think that a self-propelled vehicle was envisioned as early as the mid-18th century.

Along with the nearby 1897 Avion no 3, a wonderfully whimsical design by Clément Ader based on the ergonomics of a bat, the Fardier de Cugnot illustrates the advanced thinking of French engineers.

The Room of Echoes is a single extraordinary space in a museum that, with Foucault's pendulum, an early chemistry laboratory, 19th-century motors, French flying machines, a glass lion, a room full of architectural models, and a scaled-down replica of the Statue of Liberty, demands many visits to take it all in.

**Address** 60 rue Réaumur, 75003 Paris, +33 (0)1 53 01 82 63, www.arts-et-metiers.net | **Getting there** Metro to Arts-et-Métiers (Lines 3, 11) or Réaumur-Sébastopol (Line 4); bus 20, 38, 75 to Arts-et-Métiers | **Hours** Tue–Thu 10am–6pm, Fri 10am–9pm, Sat & Sun 10am–6pm | **Tip** The Line 11 platform of the Arts-et-Métiers metro station has a steampunk vibe reminiscent of much of the 19th-century industrial machinery found inside the museum.

# 8 Atelier des Lumières

*360 degrees of art and music*

What if Vincent Van Gogh had been alive in the 21st century instead of the 19th? How would his art appear today, and would he be a traditional painter or a digital film creator? These are questions you might ponder of all the artists presented at the Atelier des Lumières.

The Atelier is housed in the former 19th-century Plichon iron foundry and takes unique advantage of the space's size and shape. 10-meter-high (33-foot-high) walls serve as large canvasses, and big open spaces accommodate crowds without obstructing the views. Circular rooms – and even a submerged pool – create unique screens for projecting art. New expositions open once or twice yearly and feature reconstructions of the work of iconic artists like Cézanne, Kandinsky, Dali, and Klimt. A typical show encompasses 45 nonstop minutes of movement and sound pairing each artist's paintings with different genres of music from classical to pop.

The art itself has been digitized, and the layers within a painting are often separated so that a landscape painting becomes a video of moving skies and waving wheat, or pieces of images from multiple paintings are combined into new visuals. Speakers and video projectors are cleverly hidden in the pitch-black ceiling rafters, while every square centimeter of the walls and floors (and visitors) is covered with art that moves in rhythm with the music.

Make sure that you do not stay in one spot. The experience changes as you move about the foundry, sit down on a bench or the floor, enter the circular room, or observe everything from the gallery. Parents are encouraged to let their children chase the colorful art across the floors.

The Atelier des Lumières provides a new way to experience well-known artists, and every show also highlights a short, experimental video. It is perfect for today's overstimulated senses and short attention spans.

**Address** 38 rue Saint-Maur, 75011 Paris, +33 (0)1 80 98 46 00, www.atelier-lumieres.com, sav@culturespaces.com | **Getting there** Metro to Rue Saint-Maur (Line 3), Saint-Ambroise (Line 9); bus 46 to Chemin Vert, 69 to Chemin Vert-Parmentier | **Hours** See website for seasonal hours | **Tip** One block away beside Square Maurice Gardette sits Caméléon, a beautiful corner boutique full of antique finds, original creations, and other little treasures (20 rue du Général Guilhem, www.cameleonparis.com).

# 9 Balzac House

*Discovering a universal author*

Honoré de Balzac (1799–1850) lived in this house from 1840 to 1847, and it is here where he corrected *The Human Comedy*. You will see the author's office, possessions, and portraits of him and his characters. He is one of the most translated authors in the world because his works provide answers to important societal questions relevant to his time and our own. Balzac is not just a 19th-century writer, but a writer for all time.

A workaholic, Balzac went to bed at 6pm and awoke at 1am to work. He took his daily nap from 8am to 9am, and then he returned to work until 3pm before taking a three hour respite. To say that coffee helped keep him awake would be an understatement, and, in fact, he died of complications from apparently drinking 50 cups of coffee or more per day. One room in the house describes his writing process. He wrote the initial draft in pen, erased a few things, and then sent it to the printer. The typographer would set the text one character at a time and send it to print. After receiving the first draft, Balzac would cross out a few lines, add annotations, modify the order, and double the text. The process would start over again. Some pages were rewritten 30 times.

Balzac's working method is a good indication of how he became a literary giant. He was self-taught. After finishing a degree in law, he explained to his parents that the profession did not interest him, and he instead planned to become a writer. His father offered to support him for a year. During that year, Balzac isolated himself and wrote a play and some poems. A family friend, an academician, read the work and advised the aspiring writer, "My young friend, forget poetry and forget the theater as well." Balzac took the man at his word and decided to write novels. His early efforts were quite heavy-handed, and it took him ten years of hard work before becoming a great writer.

Address 47 rue Raynouard, 75016 Paris, +33 (0)1 55 74 41 80, www.maisondebalzac.paris.fr | Getting there Metro to Passy (Line 6), La Muette (Line 9); bus 32 to Place de Passy, 70 to les Vignes-Boulainvilliers, 72 to Lamballe Ankara | Hours Tue–Sun 10am–6pm | Tip Go see the building at 13 and 19 Rue Raynouard designed by the architect Louis Duhayon in 1931. Duhayon also designed the Royal Monceau and the Plaza Athénée, in 1920 and 1936 respectively.

# 10 Basilica of Saint Denis

*The final resting place of French royalty*

The Basilica of Saint Denis just north of Paris is home to an astonishingly rich history dating back to the 3rd-century tomb of Saint Denis and a Carolingian crypt from the time of Charlemagne. In the first half of the 12th century, the Abbot Suger built the façade and apse of the Basilica in the new Gothic style. Aided by new building techniques such as the flying buttress, the Basilica was completed in the 13th century.

In addition to the distinction of being the first Gothic cathedral, the site became site for royal burials, starting with King Dagobert in 639. Between the 10th and 19th centuries, all but three French kings were buried in Saint Denis; it is the final burial place for over 70 kings and queens of France. The necropolis is noted for its magnificent funerary sculpture in which the remains are placed beneath an effigy of the deceased in a lying position. Earlier effigies are relatively simple stone figures, whereas later ones better resemble the deceased. The marble tombs of Renaissance-era royalty boast two levels. Particularly extraordinary tombs were created for François I and Louis XII with Anne de Bretagne. Look for the exquisite detailing of the lace and damask on the effigies of Henry II and Catherine de Medici.

The French Revolution led to the destruction of several tombs and the removal of their remains – the tombs of Henry IV, Louis XIV, and Louis XV remain empty today. After Louis XVIII became king in 1814, the decapitated remains of Louis XVI and Marie Antoinette were exhumed and entombed in the basilica. Their monumental effigies resemble what they might have looked like on the day of their coronation, including their fine jewels.

The royal tombs have been open as a museum since 1875. Today, you can learn about the history of Saint Denis, Gothic architecture, and French royalty in a singular, spectacular setting.

**Address** 1 rue de la Légion d'Honneur, 93200 Saint-Denis, +33 (0)1 48 09 83 54, www.saint-denis-basilique.fr, basilique-saint-denis@monuments-nationaux.fr | **Getting there** Metro to Basilique de Saint-Denis (Line 13); bus 153, 253 to Légion d'Honneur, 239 to Médiathèque | **Hours** See website for seasonal hours | **Tip** The Expiatory Chapel dedicated to Louis XVI and Marie Antoinette is located on the site of the former Madeleine Cemetery where they were buried after their execution in 1793 (29 Rue Pasquier, www.chapelle-expiatoire-paris.fr).

# 11 Belmondo Museum

*Beautiful sculpture in an amazing setting*

Paul Belmondo, the father of actor Jean-Paul Belmondo, was a neo-classical sculptor who grew up in Algiers before moving to Paris in the 1920s. He received several awards in the pre-war period and later joined the faculty of the National School of Fine Arts and became a member of the Institute of France. His family gifted their collection to the city of Boulogne-Billancourt, which opened the museum in 2010 in the Château de Buchillot, an 18th-century folly that was formerly part of the nearby Château Rothschild.

The museum offers a tour of Belmondo's art, starting with a recreation of his atelier in the entrance building. The interior of the chateau itself is a unique design that maximizes the impact of each piece. The initial spaces take advantage of bright light and white walls to frame full-body stone sculptures done in the *taille directe*method, or direct carving that does not use an intermediary model. Belmondo had a predilection for female nudes, and the entrances to rooms or hallways offer sightlines designed to direct your view onto these figures and their placement in the surrounding space. Black-painted niches are cut into the walls to take advantage of the tall ceilings as they draw your eye upward while framing busts and other sculptures.

The first-floor hallway, the final stairwell, and the top floor alter the scale of the works and introduce new materials. These spaces are built from rich wood paneling with staggered shelving and are lined with dozens of busts, many in stone but also plaster studies. It is a compelling way to display these smaller pieces.

The top floor under the eaves holds an extensive collection of Belmondo's medallions and other *bas-relief*miniatures alongside sliding drawers containing his watercolor sketches. The overall effect is a serene and unusual series of galleries in which to present an artist's work.

Address 14 rue de l'Abreuvoir, 92100 Boulogne-Billancourt, +33 (0)1 55 18 69 01, www.boulognebillancourt.com/loisirs/culture/musees/musee-paul-belmondo | Getting there Metro to Boulogne Jean-Jaurès (Line 10); bus 123 to Église de Boulogne | Hours Tue–Fri 2–6pm, Sat & Sun 11am–6pm | Tip Look for two beautiful Belmondo statues, *Jeanette*and *Apollon*,in the Grand Couvert section of the Tuileries Gardens near the children's trampolines.

# 12_BnF – Richelieu

*Epicenter of manuscripts and national treasures*

Following its reopening in 2022 after a 12-year renovation, the Richelieu site of the Bibliothèque nationale de France (BnF), or National Library of France, invites visitors to explore its magnificent spaces, including the breathtaking Oval Room for reading and study, as well as areas dedicated to the permanent exhibition of the institution's treasures.

Located in the Palais Mazarin since the 18th century, in the heart of the 2nd arrondissement's Vivienne quarter, the BnF has always exhibited its collections, notably through its emblematic *Cabinet des Médailles,* or cabinet of medals. BnF's six specialized departments work together to present their objects in a unified space, showcasing pieces like the pendant of Catherine de Médicis, the cameos of Charles V, and the antiquities of the Duc de Luynes.

The visit culminates in the Mazarin Gallery. Designed by the architect François Mansart between 1644 and 1646, this gallery houses the *Grand Cameo of France* (1st century), as well as the gold bindings of the Sainte-Chapelle gospels, commissioned by King Saint Louis in the 13th century. The ceiling paintings by Giovanni Francesco Romanelli have been restored to their original splendor. Each year, the museum renews itself with a different theme, such as "Revolutions" in 2023–24. Works by astronomers, philosophers, artists, and writers depict the changes and upheavals of their time.

You'll see original manuscripts, such as Émile Zola's *L'Assommoir* and Beethoven's *Symphony No. 9.* While he was imprisoned in the Bastille in 1785, the Marquis de Sade wrote *120 Days of Sodom* on 33 sheets of paper, each 4.45 inches (11.3 centimeters) wide, glued end-to-end to form a strip that's 39 feet (11.88 meters) long and covered on both sides with microscopic writing.

The treasures of the BnF offer a journey through time, testifying to the rich cultural heritage it carefully preserves.

**Address** 5 rue Vivienne, 75002 Paris, +33 (0)1 53 79 49 49, www.bnf.fr/en/richelieu, visites@bnf.fr | **Getting there** Metro to Palais Royal-Musée du Louvre (Lines 1, 7), Bourse (Line 3), or Pyramides (Lines 7, 14); Bus 20, 29, 39, 74, 85 to Bourse, or 29 to Bibliothèque Nationale | **Hours** Tue 10am–8pm, Wed–Sun 10am–6pm | **Tip** The Opéra-Comique is one of the oldest theaters and music halls in France founded in 1714 (1 Place Boieldieu, www.opera-comique.com/en). See an opera or concert and admire this superb and charming place imbued with Parisian history and culture.

# 13 Bourdelle Museum

*Renovator of 20th-century sculpture*

Nestled in the heart of the Montparnasse district, the Bourdelle Museum is one of the last vestiges of the Paris artist communities that flourished in the late 19th and early 20th centuries. The sculptor of *Hercules the Archer* and creator of the façades of the Champs Élysées theater, Antoine Bourdelle (1861 – 1929) lived, created, and taught here from 1885 until his death. He was strongly influenced by the myths of Ancient Greece and by architectural laws, setting him apart from his contemporaries. *Hercules the Archer* helped define him as one of the renovators of 20th-century sculpture.

*Hercules the Archer* bears witness to the importance Antoine Bourdelle attached to antiquity. Created in 1910, this work enthralled critics and the public alike, and it still fascinates today. It is an expression of the artist's emancipation from the master Rodin for whom he had worked. The virtuosity of the composition can be seen in the remarkable musculature, extreme tension between the strength of the bust and of the arm, the contraction of the knee and the leg, and the perfect balance of full and negative spaces.

Antoine Bourdelle's figures express the essence of masculinity and femininity. In opposition to the strength of the male figures, his sculptures of women, like that of Pénélope, an intimate and monumental piece, is a synthesis of the women Bourdelle loved. Pénélope also reveals the artist's passion for architecture. The figure is sculpted in the image of a Doric column but with a movement in the hips and generous forms, whose folds suggest a woman's sensuality. Her eyes closed, her head resting on her hand, she makes us understand the pain of waiting for love.

You can't miss the monumental sculptures in the main hall and in the gardens. Antoine Bourdelle was also a painter, and you can enter his painting and sculpture studio, untouched since his death, as if he had just stepped out to meet a friend for dinner.

Address 18 rue Antoine Bourdelle, 75015 Paris, +33 (0)1 49 54 73 73, www.bourdelle.paris.fr | Getting there Metro to Montparnasse-Bienvenüe (Lines 4, 6, 12, 13); bus 89 to Maine Vaugirard, 58, 91, 92 to Gare Montparnasse | Hours Tue–Sun 10am–6pm | Tip Explore Espace Frans Krajcberg, an art center dedicated to the artist's passion for life, art, and the planet. Krajcberg, a Brazilian artist who lived in Paris, donated 25 artworks now on display at the center. The center supports his mission to preserve nature and protect the indigenous communities of the Amazon rainforest (21 Avenue du Maine, www.espacekrajcberg.com).

# 14 Bourse de Commerce-Pinault Collection

*Through the eyes of a contemporary art collector*

A perfect alliance between heritage and contemporary design, this majestic, circular building dates back to the 16th century. It was meticulously restored and transformed by the acclaimed Japanese architect Tadao Ando, winner of the Pritzker Prize, and features an expansive open floor plan and Le Panorama du Commerce, a stunning allegorical frieze depicting an allegory of global exchange and intercontinental connections. The interplay of light and shadow through the glass rooftop creates an atmosphere of serenity and contemplation. Here, François Pinault exhibits a selection of his personal contemporary art collection from the 1960s to the present day.

The collection includes more than 10,000 works by nearly 380 artists and consists of paintings, sculptures, videos, photographs, sound works, installations, and performances. Artists from diverse continents and multiple generations are represented, exploring the vast territories of creativity and reflecting the collector's keen interest in emerging trends.

The Bourse de Commerce is the first museum in Paris exclusively dedicated to contemporary art through a private collection. Similar to the Palazzo Grassi and the Punta della Dogana, Pinault's museum in Venice, the collection in Paris includes a dynamic program of temporary displays comprising theme-based and monographic exhibitions, as well as commissions, carte-blanche works, and onsite projects. This approach underscores the museum's commitment to providing broad support to artists in their creative endeavors.

Through this collection, you are invited to experience art through a contemporary lens with a subjective perspective shaped by Pinault's passion and enthusiasm, allowing you to engage with and comprehend the spirit of our time.

Address 2 rue de Viarmes, 75001 Paris, +33 (0)1 55 04 60 60, www.pinaultcollection.com, info.boursedecommerce@pinaultcollection.com | Getting there Metro to Louvre-Rivoli (Line 1), Les Halles (Line 2); bus 74, 85 to Bourse de Commerce, 21, 67 to Louvre-Rivoli | Hours Mon–Wed & Sat 11am–7pm, Fri 11am–9pm | Tip Visit the Colbert Gallery, built in 1823, which houses the National Institute of Art History and the National Heritage Institute and features a magnificent glass dome (4 rue Vivienne, en.parisinfo.com/paris-museum-monument/100269/Galerie-Colbert).

# 15_The Butterfly Museum

*Now you see me, now you don't!*

"Please face toward the door," directs Frédéric Ravatin, the founder of this house museum located on a picturesque hillside stairway in the 20th arrondissement. After a minute or so spent looking away and hearing the sounds of furniture being moved, you can finally turn around. Magically, his living room and unassuming home office have been transformed. The bookcases conceal floor-to-ceiling display cabinets, and all you can see is hundreds of species of thousands of butterflies.

Mr. Ravatin welcomes individuals and small groups into his home to tell his life story and share his passion for butterflies. He caught his first butterfly at the age of six and has since collected species from throughout France and the world.

In his career, he designs exhibit spaces, and this is evident in the displays for his collection. The display cabinets are actually nested shelving units, and each time he unfolds a part of the cabinets, another layer of butterflies is revealed. You learn about his favorite species and how the shape of butterfly wings displayed in a collection differs from their position in flight. He tells stories of past collecting trips and teaches you about butterfly anatomy and the source of different colors and patterns.

Then he clears work clutter off two desks to reveal them as custom display cases – even the legs have butterflies. Smaller individual trays highlight some of the largest and most spectacular species he owns. In addition to the mounted collection, he has plans for a living butterfly habitat in the outdoor garden.

At the end of your tour, Ravatin subtly illustrates why the butterfly can be so elusive when you are searching for it. When they are still and their wings are closed, they almost disappear into the background, only to burst into existence when they open. "J'existe, je n'existe pas. J'existe, je n'existe pas," he chants.

**Address** 4 rue Géo Chavez, 75020 Paris, +33 (0)1 44 87 00 44, www.musee-du-papillon.fr | **Getting there** Metro to Porte de Bagnolet (Line 3); tramway to Porte de Bagnolet (Line 3b); bus 76, 102, 351 to Porte de Bagnolet | **Hours** By appointment only | **Tip** The museum entrance is part way up the rue du Pére Prosper Enfantin, a public stairway leading to the Campagne de Paris. This hilltop neighborhood comprises cobblestone streets and one and two-story houses built in the early 20th century for workers of modest means.

# 16 Carnavalet Museum

*The stunning arc of Parisian history*

Between 2017 and 2021, the Musée Carnavalet underwent an extensive restoration of every space, object, and painting. The updates allow the Carnavalet to exhibit a timeline of Parisian history from the Mesolithic age to the recent pandemic shutdowns. In addition, there are thoughtful touches, such as multilingual signage at different heights, little red balloons that indicate information for kids, and inscriptions for Braille readers.

The result is a fascinating collection in a bright and welcoming space.

The storming of the Bastille prison on July 14, 1789 is considered the start of the French Revolution. Along with the Tennis Court Oath and Declaration of the Rights of Man, the execution of Louis XVI and Marie Antoinette, and the subsequent Reign of Terror, the Bastille is a lasting symbol of the political and social changes of this era.

Shortly after the Bastille was overtaken, memorabilia, publications, and dramatic presentations of the structure were immediately created and helped to cement the symbolism of the prison and the event. Many of these items are on display in the rooms covering the revolutionary period. The rope ladder supposedly used by writer Jean Henri Latude to escape from the prison is displayed beneath his portrait that includes the same ladder. Other items on display include cell keys, locks, and prisoner shackles.

Perhaps the most intriguing object in this collection is a stone maquette of the Bastille during the prison's demolition. The builder and entrepreneur Pierre-François Palloy was given the contract to demolish the prison, and he used the opportunity to create a range of products he sold as relics. He commissioned 83 scale copies of the Bastille carved from stones recovered from the demolition. These maquettes were distributed throughout France, and they show that even revolutions have their souvenirs.

Address 16 rue des Francs Bourgeois, 75003 Paris, +33 (0)1 44 59 58 58, www.carnavalet.paris.fr | Getting there Metro to Saint Paul (Line 1), Chemin Vert (Line 8); bus 29 to Payenne, 69, 76, 96 to Saint Paul | Hours Tue–Sun 10am–6pm | Tip Look for the gold medallions that outline the original location of the prison in the sidewalk between rue de la Bastille and rue Saint-Antoine on the west side of Place de la Bastille.

# 17 Cartier Foundation

*A vision of living contemporary art*

Founded in 1984, the Cartier Foundation for Contemporary Art is a unique example of corporate sponsorship in France. Installed in a remarkable glass building designed by the architect Jean Nouvel, its mission is to promote contemporary creation and facilitate the dissemination of knowledge by forming a significant art collection. Thanks to the foundation's support, more than 2,000 works have been created by 500 artists from 50 different nations.

What sets the Cartier Foundation apart is its commitment to fostering dynamic exchanges with artists by commissioning works that serve as the bedrock of its sponsorship. Major names in contemporary art, as well as emerging artists, are exhibited here, and visitors can view pieces that have not been exhibited anywhere else. Exhibitions at the Cartier Foundation are curated to express a vision of living contemporary art, and you can be sure to encounter the unexpected.

All forms of contemporary creation are considered here, including design, fashion, painting, photography, and architecture. The foundation puts on four solo or collective exhibitions per year covering themes that touch on hot topics in today's society. For example, a past exhibition was dedicated to the Yanomamis, an indigenous community in the Amazon, intending to raise awareness about threats to biodiversity. Sponsored by the foundation, Western artists, including Tony Oursler, Adriana Varejão, and Raymond Depardon, traveled to the Amazon to meet with the Yanomami people. The artists drew on their contact with this community to create works for the exhibition. The objective was to provide visibility to populations often excluded from the art world and share their unique vision of the world with the broader public. Additionally, the foundation provides opportunities for the public to engage with artists directly and attend captivating shows.

Address 261 boulevard Raspail, 75014 Paris, +33 (0)1 42 18 56 50, www.fondationcartier.com, info.reservation@fondation.cartier.com | Getting there Metro to Raspail (Lines 4, 6); bus 68 to Edgard Quinet, 38 to Saint Vincent de Paul | Hours Tue 11am–10pm, Wed–Sun 11am–8pm | Tip Take a stroll through the nearby Montparnasse cemetery where Charles Baudelaire and Guy de Maupassant are buried (3 Boulevard Edgar Quinet).

# 18 Centquatre-Paris

*Living art spontaneously*

The Centquatre-Paris, an art venue of the City of Paris, occupies an unusual space in the 19th arrondissement: a former funeral home spanning 39,000 square meters (420,000 square feet) that sets the tone for the center's avant-garde spirit. The Centquatre-Paris is a residence for the creation, production, and promotion of art for artists from all over the world – and for the general public too. Art in all its current forms and disciplines is fully represented here, thanks to artist residencies, as well as popular and contemporary programming. This is a vibrant, living space, where you are enticed to explore, ponder, engage, and participate in activities beyond traditional exhibitions or shows.

The idea of Director José-Manuel Gonçalves is to provide artists with tools and a space where they can forge a relationship with the public. Exhibitions here are never static. As dynamic displays, they generate questions and elicit cross-disciplinary reflections and conversations that can take the form of screenings, lectures, round tables, and other events.

The exhibitions here are not what visitors traditionally find in a museum. You may come to see one particular show and find yourself enticed toward something entirely different as well. You may encounter young designers and emerging artists showing their work here. Artists can interact directly with the public, and scholars are sometimes invited to provide alternative perspectives. This is a spontaneous way of experiencing art.

Thanks to funding from the City of Paris, entry into the Centquatre-Paris is free. The open space is flanked by shops and eateries. You'll also find activities for children, and art experiences. People from all walks of life can be seen here – young and old, art professionals and laypeople. The strength of the Centquatre-Paris lies in the people populating the space; they are what makes it so special.

**Address** 5 rue Curial, 75019 Paris, +33 (0)1 53 35 50 00, www.104.fr, contact@104.fr | **Getting there** Metro to Riquet (Line 7); bus 35, 45, 519 to Riquet | **Hours** Tue–Fri noon–7pm, Sat & Sun 11am–7pm | **Tip** Have fun at the very cool Grande Fantaisie barge, an associative cultural center in the 19th with varied artistic programming, workshops, and other events. A creative and friendly place open to all, as well as a place to eat and even dance! (9 quai de l'Oise, Paris 75019)

# 19_Cernuschi Museum

*A visionary's collection of Asian art*

The Cernuschi Museum, located in the private mansion of Henri Cernuschi (1821–1896), is an invitation to travel. A wealthy investor of Italian origin, Henri Cernuschi bought a parcel of land in the then-booming Plaine Monceau district and commissioned an architect to build a house that reflected his aesthetic. A visionary, his idea was to create a home/museum for his collection of more than 5,000 pieces of art that he brought back from China and Japan between 1871 and 1873. He wanted to make his collection available to everyone. From 1875 onwards, the collection could be visited by appointment, and the owner himself was happy to act as a guide. Gustave Moreau and Émile Zola were among his regular visitors.

Cernuschi resided here until his death and bequeathed his collection and mansion to the City of Paris. The recently redesigned spaces capture the intimate atmosphere intended by its founder. A section is dedicated to the history of Henri Cernuschi's collection, which began during the collector's journey in Asia. Japan was his first stop on a trip that also included China, Ceylon, and India. He shipped numerous crates containing several thousand items back to France. He moved from one region to another without ever staying for more than three months in the same country. His collection captivated both artists and manufacturers of the time, exerting a significant influence on the Art Nouveau period. He acquired the *Buddha of Meguro*, which was, in his words, "an unparalleled find."

Visitors to the museum are immersed in a unique history providing a panoramic view of Chinese art that spans dynasties, from prehistoric times until the 21st century. Exceptional bronzes and ceramics are on display too. The museum opens up to other geographical areas in East Asia as well, offering a program of temporary exhibitions that allows visitors to make new discoveries.

**Address** 7 avenue Vélasquez, 75008 Paris, +33 (0)1 53 96 21 50, www.cernuschi.paris.fr | **Getting there** Metro to Monceau (Line 2), Villiers (Lines 2, 3); bus 20, 30, 93 to Malesherbes-Courcelles, 84 to Ruysdaël | **Hours** Tue–Sun 10am–6pm | **Tip** The Cernuschi Museum overlooks Parc Monceau, which was commissioned by the Duke of Chartres in the 17th century. It is one of the most elegant gardens in Paris (35 boulevard de Courcelles, Monceau).

# 20 Chana Orloff Atelier-Museum

*Sculptures that come to life*

The Chana Orloff Atelier-Museum opened permanently to the public in 2019 thanks to the artist's grandchildren. Orloff was already a well-known sculptor in the 1920s when she hired Auguste Perret to design her studio/residence located in Villa Seurat, a charming street of artists' homes in the 14th arrondissement. Perret captured the essence of geometry and harmonious spaces here, harnessing light to create a unique environment for her artistic work and exhibitions.

Orloff's granddaughter will invite you into the studio to immerse yourself in the artist's private space and surrender to her powerful sculptures. Born in Russia in 1888, Orloff stands as one of the most celebrated artists of the School of Paris. The clean lines, geometry, sensuality, and density of her work stands in contrast with the trajectory of her life, which is both moving and painful. As a woman, a mother, a Jew, and a Russian immigrant living in France, her journey resonates deeply, as her sculptures bear witness to her humanity.

Orloff began her career by sculpting portraits of famous friends and notable figures, such as Guillaume Apollinaire, Amedeo Modigliani, Anaïs Nin, and many others. Her portraits, inspired by cubism and primitivism, are sculpted in plaster, wood, bronze, and marble. However, her artistic repertoire extended beyond portraiture. Orloff explored various themes, including the representation of women and animals that held a deep significance for her. Initially, her pieces featured a highly stylized and smooth aesthetic. Later, she added texture through the medium and her own fingerprints in a style that is still figurative but more abstract. The collection on display provides a comprehensive overview of the diverse and evocative nature of Orloff's art.

Address 7 bis Villa Seurat, 75014 Paris, +33 (0)1 60 92 22 17, www.chana-orloff.org, info@chana-orloff.org | Getting there Metro to Alésia (Line 4); RER B to Denfert-Rochereau; bus 68 to Alésia-Général Leclercq | Hours By appointment only | Tip Take a stroll around Villa Seurat to discover two dozen studios/homes of artists, painters, architects, sculptors, ceramicists, and writers who elected to take up residence here.

# 21_City of Architecture and Patrimony

*The Tour de France of French buildings*

The City of Architecture is a surprising experience, a veritable tour of France's most sensational buildings from the Middle Ages to the present day. This unique venue is located in the Paris Wing of the Chaillot Palace that was built for the International Exhibition of 1937. Here, you will find full-sized casts of sculptures and architectural fragments and models.

Upon entering the gallery of casts on the first floor, you'll stroll through one portal after the next. You will gaze upon ornate tympanums, pillars, and many more architectural details.

The architect Eugène Viollet-le-Duc (1814–1879) conceived the idea of a museum of comparative sculpture, focusing on French monuments as a way of promoting knowledge and awareness of medieval architecture. He launched a campaign of plaster casting throughout France to assemble life-sized architectural elements in one place.

This collection offers priceless insights to archaeologists, as it has guided renovation projects of churches, cathedrals, and abbeys that have suffered damage, including Notre Dame Cathedral. The museum has models of the cathedral's frame and the spire that collapsed in the great fire of 2019.

The second floor is dedicated to the evolution of architecture throughout the 19th and 20th centuries. Look for a model of the City of Paris that shows changes to the city made by Haussmann, and the reconstruction at scale of an apartment from Le Corbusier's Cité Radieuse. The museum has also enriched its collection with a gallery of reproductions of wall paintings and French stained-glass windows from the Romanesque period to the dawn of the Renaissance. View the ornate dome of Cahors, and visit the 12th-century crypts of Saint-Nicolas de Tavant Church that cannot be seen in real life.

**Address** 1 place du Trocadéro et du 11 Novembre, 75016 Paris, +33 (0)1 58 51 52 00, www.citedelarchitecture.fr | **Getting there** Metro to Trocadéro (Lines 6, 9); bus 20, 22, 32, 63 to Trocadéro | **Hours** Wed–Mon 11am–7pm | **Tip** Admire gilded bronze statues from the 1937 Exhibition as you stroll through the courtyard of the Palais de Chaillot. Slowly make your way to the plaza for a breathtaking view of the Eiffel Tower.

# 22 City of Economics

*Come for the architecture, stay for the economics*

Economics might not seem to be a terribly interesting subject for a museum – at least not until you visit the City of Economics in the Hotel Gaillard. This museum is actually three attractions, and, as the staff suggests, it can be experienced as three equally fascinating visits.

Your first visit is to a historical home featuring Renaissance architecture. The Hôtel Gaillard was built by banker Emile Gaillard in the late 19th century as a neo-Renaissance masterpiece based on the Chateau du Blois. You'll visit the private family spaces, including Gaillard's bathroom with its huge safe. Each room features historic woodwork, chimneys, and other architectural pieces from his art collection. You'll see the salon where he staged his famous 1885 costume ball. And you'll don a mixed-reality headset and follow his ghost around the home to learn about his friendship with Frédéric Chopin. On your second visit, you'll learn about economics via a series of exhibits covering topics such as trade, currencies, markets, regulation, and economic crises.

Through traditional displays, interactive games, and scholarly debates between experts, visitors of different ages and education levels can learn about each topic in the way that suits them best. One unusual experience allows you to enter a conference room and role-play different countries negotiating with each other.

Your final visit brings you into the early 20th century, when the mansion was transformed into a commercial branch of the Bank of France, complete with an art deco-style teller area. After doing some imaginary banking, walk down the small spiral staircase with a whimsical winged Gaillard carved into its base to the area outside the bank vault, which is actually a retracting bridge over a moat. Then enter the huge vault with thousands of individual safe deposit boxes and create a Euro bill with your own image.

Address 1 place du Général Catroux, 75017 Paris, +33 (0)1 86 47 10 10, www.citeco.fr | Getting there Metro to Malesherbes (Line 3), Monceau (Line 2); bus 20, 93 to Place du Général Catroux, 30 to Malesherbes-Courcelles | Hours Tue–Fri 2–6pm, Sat 2–7pm, Sun 2–6pm | Tip The Place du Général Catroux has several notable monuments and buildings in and around it, including statues of Alexandre Dumas (father and son) and Sarah Bernhardt (boulevard Malesherbes at avenue de Villiers).

# 23 City of Science and Industry

*STEM for the entire family*

Here's one for kids and their favorite grown-ups. The cavernous City of Science and Industry invites exploration with numerous permanent exhibits and a diverse selection of temporary expositions throughout the year. Whether your interest is technology, astronomy, transportation, or pure science, this is the type of museum that requires multiple visits just to scratch the surface.

The museum is organized on several levels starting with the Cité des Enfants with two age-based areas dedicated to very young children getting their first exposure to their place in the world and interacting with other children, as well as basic physical phenomena. The second area includes more advanced and autonomous activities for kids up to 12 years old.

Adults can really get involved by both learning new things and reacquainting themselves with scientific knowledge that they may have learned as children but forgotten after they left school. Families can watch a show in the classic planetarium, explore the brain and test their own capabilities, and learn about global warming and what can be done to reverse it in the future. On your next visit, learn about satellites and the universe, genetics, and multiple modes of transport, and then tour an old attack submarine.

The mathematics exhibit exemplifies the museum's focus on learning by doing. Games and models illustrate concepts in geometry, movement, and numbers. Play a colorful round of three-dimensional tic-tac-toe. Predict the route balls will take through a Gaiton board. Dip a metal shape into soapy water to explore minimal surfaces. Learn about unpredictable Brownian movement. And use a *chaoteur*to follow the random trail of a pendulum suspended between three magnets. You'll be amazed how much you can learn in a few hours of play.

Address 30 avenue Corentin-Cariou, 75019 Paris, www.cite-sciences.fr, infocontact@universcience.fr | Getting there Metro to Porte de la Villette (Line 7); tramway T3b to Porte de la Villette; bus 71, 139, 150, 152 to Porte de la Villette | Hours Tue–Sat 9:30am–6pm, Sun 9:30am–7pm | Tip For more scientific discovery, visit the temporary home of the Palais de la Découverte in Parc André-Citroën (186 rue Saint Charles, www.palais-decouverte.fr).

# 24 Clemenceau Museum

*Publisher, collector, adventurer, and statesman*

Perhaps you know Georges Clemenceau (1841–1929) as the prime minister who negotiated the Treaty of Versailles. Or maybe you remember the picture of him exiting the negotiations, or his earlier visits to the front during World War I in his large coat and hat. You may have learned about the 1905 law enshrining the separation of church and state. The Clemenceau Museum pays homage to the great statesman.

In this house museum, you'll feel the sensation of being part of his world. This was his home for the last 30+ years of his life. The upper level of this two-floor museum lays out Clemenceau's history in classic fashion as a series of dates, events, and accomplishments. He was a world traveler who lived in the United States, visited South America, and traveled throughout Asia in his 80s. He was a journalist who published several newspapers throughout his life. He was the editor-in-chief at *L'Aurore*who ran Emile Zola's famous open letter to President Faure, "J'accuse…!" And of course, he was the politician who served in the National Assembly and twice as prime minister.

On the bottom floor, his residence has been left almost exactly as it was when Clemenceau lived in it and conducted his affairs. The 4,000 books he kept still line the library and hallway shelves alongside a collection of artwork and photos, including those of his friends Claude Monet and Auguste Rodin. The huge U-shaped desk in his library still has its Buddha, its teapots, and other objects resting in their customary places. In the bedroom, there is his bed with his slippers neatly by its side and his robe laid over a nearby chair. Across the room is a small desk where you can imagine him writing letters or plays. His inkwell, a bowl of sand (he never used a blotter), and various objects of chinoiserie remain as they were. And a calendar still shows the date of his passing in 1929.

**Address** 8 rue Benjamin Franklin, 75116 Paris, +33 (0)1 45 20 53 41, www.musee-clemenceau.fr, info@musee-clemenceau.fr | **Getting there** Metro to Passy (Line 6), Trocadéro (Lines 6, 9); bus 32 to Scheffer | **Hours** Tue–Sat 2–5:30pm | **Tip** The Jardin Clemenceau, designed by Alphonse Alphand in 1859 and now next to the Petit Palais, houses a statue of the statesman (Place Clemenceau and avenue Winston Churchill).

# 25 Cluny Museum

*The fantastic world of the Middle Ages*

The Middle Ages are often maligned, often thought of as a period of disease, war, poverty, and violence. However, a visit to the recently renovated Musée de Cluny will challenge these preconceptions. Medieval Europe here is a fantasy world full of mysteries, extraordinary tales, and unbridled imagination.

Alexandre Du Sommerard (1779–1842) understood this and dedicated himself to his passion. He set up residence in the Hôtel de Cluny, amassing a remarkable collection of more than 1,500 objects. It is thanks to him that the Cluny Museum exists today to offer a captivating journey through centuries of history, from Gallo-Roman antiquity to the dawn of the Renaissance.

In the Middle Ages, people knew how to tell stories, not necessarily in books, but woven into tapestries, like the museum's six famous *Lady and the Unicorn* tapestries. One of the museum's most beautiful masterpieces is an ivory box called *L'Assaut du Château d'Amour*, which depicts scenes of courtly love. Women defend a castle with flowers against the onslaught of knights. The box is further adorned with additional scenes, including the story of Aristotle mocked by Alexander the Great's lover, and the tale of Tristan and Isolde being observed by King Mark at the fountain.

Medieval artists had a taste for symbolic imagery. It is often said that they lacked the ability to draw realistically. More likely, their aesthetic was simply unconcerned with creating likenesses. A painting of the Madonna nursing her baby surrounded by praying angels depicts Christ as an adult in miniature. According to the artists of the time, as the child is divine, he could not be represented as a fragile infant. The magic of medieval art is the use of a composition system that leaves room for multiple interpretations. It is up to you to guess, decipher, and look at the works of art with fresh and curious eyes.

Address 28 rue du Sommerard, 75005 Paris, +33 (0)1 53 73 78 00, www.musee-moyenage.fr, contact.musee-moyenage@culture.gouv.fr | Getting there Metro to Odéon (Line 4), Cluny-La Sorbonne (Line 10); bus 63, 86, 87 to Cluny | Hours Tue–Sun 9:30–6:15pm | Tip Visit the Saint-Etienne-du-Mont church and look for its finely carved, 16th-century stone jube, one of the last existing in Paris (Place Sainte Genevieve, www.saintetiennedumont.fr).

# 26 Cognacq-Jay Museum

*A light and carefree world*

The Cognacq-Jay Museum's collection represents the vision of two 19th-century collectors, husband and wife Théodore-Ernest Cognacq (1839–1928) and Marie-Louise Jaÿ (1836–1925), who were captivated by the art and styles of the 18th century. This collection represents the fascination of the era for 18th-century decorative arts and serves as a reflection of the 19th-century obsession with past styles. You'll get a glimpse into the luxurious lifestyle of the privileged class during that time, characterized by a carefree and libertine aesthetic.

The collection is varied and diverse, encompassing furniture, paintings, and decorative arts. The furniture is small and refined, and the paintings often represent genre scenes expressing femininity and delicacy. Iconic 18th-century painter Robert Hubert presents an idealized vision, while Jean-Honoré Fragonard's works exude sensuality. The furniture itself is a marvel, with hidden drawers and intricate details that arouse curiosity and admiration.

One unique feature of the museum is the vast collection of over 200 *objets de vertu*, or small luxury items, from the period, making it one of the largest groupings in France. These tiny, ingenuous masterpieces are exquisite and precious, as they exemplify invention and fantasy.

During the 18th century, such objects were in vogue and often exchanged as tokens of friendship or love, often accompanied with messages. They were made of gold or enamel and embellished with precious stones, mother-of-pearl, or ivory. Whether utilitarian or collectible, these items offer insights into the social practices of the time. The collection features a fly box (a cosmetic accessory with small black dots used to enhance the complexion), a dance card, writing and sewing kits, a tobacco box, and a perfume gun. The Cognacq-Jay Museum transports us into a world of elegance, fantasy, and coquetry.

Address 8 rue Elzévir, 75003 Paris, +33 (0)1 40 27 07 21, www.museecognacqjay.paris.fr | Getting there Metro to Saint Paul (Line 1); bus 29 to Turenne-Saint-Gilles, 69, 76, 96 to Saint Paul | Hours Tue–Sun 10am–6pm | Tip Discover the Passage de l'Ancre, one of Paris' best kept secrets and a true haven of peace and unparalleled charm in the 3rd arrondissement (223 rue Saint-Martin).

# 27 The Conciergerie

*The fascinating history of a unique palace*

The Conciergerie is a must-visit destination for enthusiasts of French history. As you step inside, you feel the weight of its past. A relic from the reign of the Capetians, this Gothic palace is one of the finest examples of 14th-century civil architecture. Amazingly, the Hall of the Guards, the Hall of Men-at-Arms, and the kitchens are still intact.

Neglected by the kings of France in the 14th century, the palace was subsequently used as a courthouse and prison. During the French Revolution of 1789, the Conciergerie became the seat of the revolutionary tribunal, and its prisons became a symbol of the Reign of Terror. Marie Antoinette was imprisoned here for more than 70 days before being guillotined.

The HistoPad is a complimentary device visitors can use to embark on an immersive journey through the medieval and revolutionary chambers as they were during their respective periods. The Hall of the Men-at-Arms, the largest surviving medieval city hall in Europe, was built between 1302 and 1313. It served as a refectory for up to 2,000 members of the king's staff, and the medieval kitchens with their massive fireplaces are equally spectacular.

Upon entering the rooms dedicated to the French Revolution, you cannot help but be deeply moved by the corridors once trodden by prisoners. You'll also see the caretaker's office, the chamber where the condemned had their hair cut, and the cells, including the windowless room where Marie Antoinette was incarcerated, so dark that she went blind while inside. A dress and a pair of shoes, her last possessions, are on display. A poignant painting by the queen's portraitist Alexander Kucharsky presents an unfamiliar side of this famous historical figure. The public personality and arbiter of elegance fades behind a woman's suffering. Her face is pale and tense, her eyes drowned in sadness. She inspires respect and sympathy.

Address 2 boulevard du Palais, Paris 75001, +33 (0)1 53 40 60 80, www.paris-conciergerie.fr | Getting there Metro to Cité (Line 4), Châtelet (Lines 1, 7, 11, 14); bus 21, 38, 47, 96 to Cité-Palais de Justice | Hours Daily 9:30am–6pm | Tip Visit the Sainte Chapelle, a radiant gothic jewel built over seven years to house Christian relics, including Jesus Christ's crown of thorns, acquired by Saint Louis (10 boulevard de Palais, www.sainte-chapelle.fr).

# 28 Counterfeiting Museum

*Is everything a fake?*

When you hear the word counterfeit, you may think immediately of the knockoff Louis Vuitton bags sold in the Tuileries, fake Rolex watches sold on Canal Street in New York City, infamous recreations of Rembrandt paintings, or North Korean-made US$100 dollar bills. The Counterfeiting Museum, run by the Union des Fabricants, is here to assure you that the problem is far worse.

Almost every product made today is a candidate for counterfeiting, and these imitations are found globally. A new Silk Road for counterfeits starts with their manufacture in East Asia and makes its way west via rail, road, and sea.

The union was started in the 19th century to fight against German pharmaceutical counterfeits. Today, it works to protect intellectual property and monitor the markets. The museum serves to educate the public on the depth and breadth of the problem. It starts with defining exactly what counterfeiting is: an infringement of intellectual property rights by reproducing, imitating, or using a trademark or patent without the owner's consent. There are several categories of counterfeits. Some are blatant copies, while others simply appear similar enough to another product to confuse the consumer into thinking that it's the original product.

This small museum shows a diverse array of counterfeits alongside their real counterparts. You'll see handbags, perfume, clothing, and shoes, of course, but also alcohol, tennis racquets, condoms, sunscreen, medicines, small electronics, children's toys, chainsaws, and pens. The list goes on and on. Even rearview mirrors for cars are counterfeited.

It's almost a relief to visit a last small room of classic art forgeries, such as the copied work of a master painter or the unauthorized Auguste Rodin sculpture casting. Given the vast number of mundane objects being counterfeited worldwide, these art fakes are almost elegant.

Address 16 rue de la Faisanderie, 75116 Paris, +33 (0)1 56 26 14 03, musee-contrefacon.com, musee@unifab.com | Getting there Metro to Porte Dauphine (Line 2); RER C to Avenue Foch; bus PC to Porte Dauphine | Hours Mon–Sat 2–5:30pm | Tip To see some authentic luxury goods, head up Avenue Foch and across the Place Charles de Gaulle to the Louis Vuitton store on the Champs-Élysées (11 Avenue des Champs-Élysées, www.louisvuitton.com).

# 29 Curie Museum

*The laboratory of a French heroine*

Following the death of her husband Pierre in 1906, Marie Curie (1867–1934) took over his position at the Sorbonne and dedicated the rest of her life to the study of radioactivity. She earned her second Nobel Prize in 1911 for the isolation of pure radium, and in 1914, she opened the Curie Laboratory of the Radium Institute to find uses for radium in the treatment of cancer.

During World War I, Curie developed mobile radiological vehicles and directed the installation of x-ray units in field hospitals. After the war, she worked to raise funds for radium research and led the activities of the institute alongside Claudius Regaud of the Pasteur Laboratory. Her daughter and son-in-law Irène and Frédéric Joliot-Curie also worked there, and they received a Nobel Prize in 1935 for the discovery of artificial radioactivity. Curie worked from this location for the rest of her career until her death in 1934.

The Radium Institute's small campus included the Curie Pavilion with physics and chemistry laboratories, and the Pasteur Pavilion for biological and medical research. Curie designed a garden between the two buildings, as well as a third building, the Petit Pavilion. Her office and a small laboratory were on the main floor of the institute, with doors that led out to a porch next to the garden. You can see these spaces today, including a life-sized, photographic cutout of Curie looking out over the garden and her namesake Marie Curie pink and gold roses.

The museum's permanent collection tells the story of the Curie family, radium and its applications, and the equipment used in the laboratories. In addition to highlighting legitimate research, the museum covers the radium craze in the 1920s and the many useless but extremely harmful products built around radium's popularity. Cue *Radium Girls*.

Look for the lead-lined box used to carry the famous gram (.035 oz) of radium Curie received from President Warren Harding on her successful first fundraising tour of the United States in 1921.

Address 1 rue Pierre et Marie Curie, 75005 Paris, +33 (0)1 56 24 55 33, musee.curie.fr | Getting there Metro to Cardinal Lemoine (Line 10), Place Monge (Line 7); RER B to Luxembourg; bus 24 to Musée et Institut Curie, 21, 27 to Saint-Jacques-Gay-Lussac | Hours Wed–Sat 1–5pm | Tip Marie et Pierre Curie are buried together in lead-lined tombs within the Panthéon (Place du Panthéon, www.paris-pantheon.fr).

# 30 Custodia Foundation

*In service to art history*

The Custodia Foundation houses the collection of Frits Lugt and Jacoba Klever in the beautiful Hôtel Turgot in the 7th arrondissement. While the foundation has a permanent collection and holds temporary exhibitions in its galleries, it is not a traditional fine arts museum. Aside from the exhibitions, the foundation does not feature galleries with art on permanent display that might appeal to the casual visitor. But a planned visit can be an extraordinary experience.

With its mission to serve art history, the foundation is a must for researchers and students, particularly those interested in Dutch and Flemish art, European drawings and prints on paper, autographed letters, collectors' stamps, art conservation, and historical frames. A spectacular study room in period décor allows visitors to view items from the collection by appointment, and the public can register to access one of the largest art research libraries in Europe. The collection contains over 20,000 prints and drawings, and the library has a particularly extensive collection of monographs and catalogues dedicated to these art forms.

For the art lover, unique temporary exhibitions are held each year. In addition to the old masters and contemporary artists like Siemen Dijkstra, the foundation has displayed a particular fondness for the work of lesser-known masters, such as French painter George Michel, Dutch impressionist Willem Bastiann Tholen, and Danish artist Christoffer Wilhelm Eckersberg. As expected, the exhibitions are comprehensive and often emphasize drawings and works on paper.

The final highlight of a visit is the guided tour of the salons and art from the collection hanging in the 18th-century private mansion. The three-story staircase, in particular, hosts a revolving selection of small, exquisitely framed landscapes hung floor to ceiling on the walls of the stairwell and landings.

Address 121 rue de Lille, 75007 Paris, +33 (0)1 47 05 75 19, www.fondationcustodia.fr, coll.lugt@fondationcustodia.fr | Getting there Metro to Assemblée Nationale (Line 12); bus 63, 73, 83, 84, 87 to Assemblée Nationale | Hours Sce website for tour and exhibition schedule | Tip Nearby, the Basilica of Saint Clotilde features one of the many organs in Paris built by the famous builder Aristide Cavaillé-Coll. It was first played by composer César Franck (23 rue Las Cases, www.sainte-clotilde.com).

# 31 Dalí Paris

*Making sense of surrealism*

Located in the heart of Montmartre, Dalí Paris displays more than 300 works from the private collection of gallery owner and collector Beniamino Levi. Levi acquired many of the pieces directly from Salvador Dalí (1904–1989). The history of the collection first began with an encounter between Dalí, one of the masters of surrealism, and Levi, who would later become the editor and curator of Dalí's sculptures. Surrealist paintings, sculptures, prints, objects, and furniture bring to life the eclectic ideas of an insatiable explorer who was passionate about atomic science, antiquity and the Renaissance, alchemy and religion.

Dalí's works are as intriguing as his personality. The museum's first room features interviews with the artist, and you are immediately drawn into his world. Of Dalí, with his famous mustache and whimsical spirit, Levi would say, "Privately, Dalí was much more than a mere buffoon (…), he took great pleasure in expressing himself in total freedom and in a surreal way, with an extraordinary vocabulary."

Throughout Dalí's oeuvre, a system of symbols becomes apparent, such as the angels or crutches that are present in his pieces. These fetish objects express the message of his art and are inspired by the obsessions of his subconscious mind. His sculptures, a major part of his work, materialize his obsessive surrealist imaginings through other symbols, such as melting watches, wading animals, and drawers.

In 1931, Dalí produced a painting that would become iconic, *The Persistence of Memory*, which explores the theme of malleable time. During the second half of his career, this motif would appear regularly and gave rise to multiple sculptures that you can see in this museum. You will also learn about Dalí's technical processes, including his use of wax as a sculpting medium and his engraving techniques for creating his works.

Address 11 rue Poulbot, 75018 Paris, +33 (0)1 42 64 40 10, www.daliparis.com | Getting there Metro to Anvers (Line 2), Abbesses (Line 12); bus 20 to Place du Tertre-Norvins | Hours Daily 10am–6pm | Tip Takc a short walk from the museum to see Dalí's home on 7 rue Beckerel. Other celebrities like Louise Michel, Nadja, and Éluard also lived on this tiny street.

# 32 Deyrolle

*The strength and fragility of the natural world*

"I've never seen a wolf up close before!" exclaims a 10-year-old boy before running down the hall into the entomology room. Moments later, you can tell from his voice that he's found the scarab beetle or perhaps a group of blue morpho butterflies. These moments of discovery bring locals and tourists to this venerable institution in Paris' 6th arrondissement.

But owner Louis Albert De Broglie also involves Deyrolle in many of his passions, conservation, biodiversity, and pedagogy among them. Deyrolle's current projects include working with public schools to teach children about climate change and environmental stewardship, preserving the various species of tomato at his chateau in the Loire Valley, planting a microfarm at Versailles, and working with the Chinese government in Sichuan province to create a new panda park.

Back on rue de Bac, take the winding stairs at the rear of the garden shop to the second floor and you enter a fascinating exhibit of taxidermy animals, artful insect displays, and Deyrolle's famous educational posters. The fabulous 19th-century décor remains in several rooms packed floor to ceiling with mammals, birds, and crustaceans. A giraffe and lion greet you at the entrance, antelope and deer line the corridors, and a peacock competes with butterflies for the title of most colorful display.

Among the animals at Deyrolle, most of which died from natural causes at zoos or nature parks, one in particular excites emotions among visitors and is a personal favorite of Deyrolle's director. It is a massive black bull with its brand still visible on its flanks.

The bull died from a heart condition, and in the location of its heart there is now a mirror box display of yellow butterflies. To Deyrolle, the display symbolizes both the force and fragility of life. The powerful can be laid low, and the small and gentle will survive.

Address 46 rue du Bac, 75007 Paris, +33 (0)1 42 22 30 07, www.deyrolle.com, contact@deyrolle.fr | Getting there Metro to rue du Bac (Line 12); bus 63, 68, 69 to rue du Bac | Hours Mon–Sat 10am–7pm | Tip Galerie Maeght, located down the block from Deyrolle, displays and sells an extensive collection of modern and contemporary art, mostly from France and Spain. Joan Miró in particular is very well represented (42 rue du Bac, www.maeght.com).

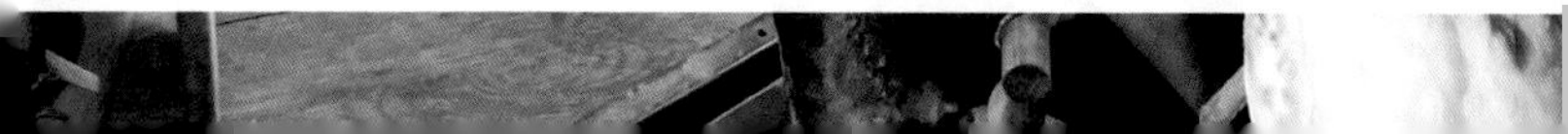

# 33 Eugène Delacroix Museum

*The master artist's private world*

Eugène Delacroix (1798–1863) was a renowned Romanticist painter known today for works such as *Liberty Leading the People*, *The Death of Sardanapalus*, and *The Lion Hunt*. But to visit his house museum at Place Furstemberg is to understand the appeal and fascination with the idea of "the lone master artist" tucked away in their sunlit atelier in a beautiful corner of Paris, focusing intensely and working diligently on their next masterpiece.

Certainly, the secluded garden behind the museum, with its scattered seating, perimeter plantings, and postage stamp lawn, is one of the most serene gems of the city. Delacroix enjoyed exclusive access to it during his time there, and he grew a variety of flowers, among them hyacinths, tulips, ranunculus, narcissus, and roses. As Delacroix himself said, "My lodgings are decidedly charming…The sight of my little garden and the pleasant appearance of my studio always accord a feeling of pleasure."

Delacroix took up residence in the apartment that is now the museum in 1857 to be closer to the Academy of Beaux-Arts and the Church of Saint Sulpice, where he painted several large chapel murals in the early 1860s. While the living space was modest, at least by today's standards, the atelier was bright and spacious with cathedral-height ceilings. It would have been perfect for large-scale works or several simultaneous projects. In his day, it housed hundreds of paintings, studies, and sketches. Today, the atelier is a highlight of an artistic visit to the museum, with its striking red walls, period furniture, two maquettes of ceiling murals, and the easels and palettes he used in his work.

The museum's collection itself is quite large, and Delacroix's work is shown in a rotating series of temporary exhibits exploring topics such as his use of light and color, his exploration of mythological themes, his love of nature, or his fascination with Morocco.

Address 6 rue de Furstemberg, 75006 Paris, +33 (0)1 44 41 86 50, www.musee-delacroix.fr, contact.musee-delacroix@louvre.fr | Getting there Metro to Saint-Germain-des-Prés (Line 4), Mabillon (Line 10); bus 39, 95 to Saint-Germain-des-Prés | Hours Wed–Mon 9:30am–5:30pm | Tip The famous Delacroix murals in the Chapel of the Holy Angels at the Church of Saint-Sulpice were wonderfully restored in 2015 (2 rue Palatine, www.paroissesaintsulpice.paris).

# 34 Eyeglasses Museum

*Meyrowitz, visionary opticians*

Emil Meyrowitz started selling eyeglasses on the streets of New York City in 1875, and he opened several shops in New York and London over the following decades. He also sold optical equipment and even hearing aids. His first shop in Paris opened in 1904 on rue Scribe, and the current atelier opened in 1922. While eyeglass styles have changed, the appearance of the shop, with its elegant period décor of mahogany walls and cabinetry, has remained the same.

Downstairs in the current atelier, a small museum provides a surprisingly comprehensive look at the history of eyeglasses. If you call ahead for an appointment, general director and curator Jean Manuel Finot will be happy to take fellow enthusiasts on an adventure through the collection.

You'll learn about Meyrowitz's involvement in World War I, when they designed eye and face protection against mustard gas. For early airplanes and automobiles with open air cockpits, they furnished some of the first goggles to protect pilots and drivers from wind and debris. Charles Lindbergh purportedly wore a pair during his 1924 flight across the Atlantic. Legend has it he came to the store afterward to celebrate his achievement.

The museum has an extensive collection of eyeglasses made from tortoiseshell, buffalo horn, and even dehydrated milk, as well as later plastic designs from designers such as Cardin, Dior, and Moschino. Jacques Chirac, Teddy Roosevelt, and Jackie Onassis were among Meyrowitz's clients, and the guestbook is a who's who of 20th-century celebrities.

The museum's greatest treasure is a pair of eyeglasses made for Claude Monet. Monet suffered from cataracts late in life, which added a yellow tint to everything he saw. His eyeglasses were fitted with blue Zeiss glass to correct his color issues. A pair of these glasses was sold at auction, and another takes pride of place in the Meyrowitz collection.

Address 5 rue de Castiglione, 75001 Paris, +33 (0)1 42 60 63 64, www.meyrowitz.paris, meyrowitz@meyrowitz.paris | Getting there Metro to Tuileries (Line 1); bus 72 to Castiglione | Hours By appointment only Mon–Fri 10am–6:30pm; Sat 10am–1pm, 2–6:30pm | Tip There is a plaque next door at 7 rue de Castiglione dedicated to Serge Lifar, a dancer and ballet master long associated with the Paris Opéra Ballet. He was condemned as a Nazi collaborator and even fought a duel with fellow choreographer George de Cuevas.

# 35_Fairground Art Museum

*Welcome to the fair! Enjoy the rides!*

Music heralds your visit to the Fairground Art Museum. Founded in 1996 by a passionate collector of fairground rides and figures, the museum invites you to experience the opulent traveling spectacles of the late 19th and early 20th centuries, starting with the grand player organ. Designed to be heard from up to 2.4 kilometers (1.5 miles) away, it called locals to an extravagant temporary building in which there were rides, performances, games, and dining – and the magic of electricity.

The museum is housed in former wine warehouses in Bercy – you can see the train tracks that used to bring casks from boats on the Seine. Pass the winged Venuses at the entrance to enjoy dozens of sculpted figures, a Venetian carnival scene, and costumed automatons singing opera with voices that shatter glass. A spiegeltent called "The Magic Mirror" promises music and dancing.

Surprisingly, you can play the fair games and ride the carousels! The traditional carousel features horses from France and Germany (you can tell by their tails), while a bowling game pits visitors against each other to move Parisian waiters along a racecourse. The player who consistently bowls a high number will see their waiter, carrying his drink tray and towel, scurry across the track to win the race.

Another star of the show is the shiny, metal Bicycle Carousel. For many 19th-century fairgoers, it was their first opportunity to ride a bicycle. Modern visitors can experience the exhilaration of a carousel whose speed is controlled by the pedaling of its riders.

Just shout out if you are feeling woozy, and a bell will tell your fellow bicyclists to slow down.

On your way out, pay your respects to Mr. Tête à Claques with a head made of leather and a scale perched on top. This sad figure has endured a lot. Fairgoers would punch his face, and the scale would measure their prowess.

**Address** 53 avenue des Terroirs de France, 75012 Paris, +33 (0)1 43 40 16 22, arts-forains.com, infos@pavillons-de-bercy.com | **Getting there** Metro to Cour St Emilion (Line 14); bus 24, 109, 111 to Terroirs de France | **Hours** Guided tours by reservation only | **Tip** After your visit to the museum, stay in the neighborhood and go shopping, have a meal, or buy tea at the nearby Bercy Village outdoor mall (28 rue François Truffaut, www.bercyvillage.com).

# 36 Fragonard Museum

*Fascinating and ghoulish veterinary science*

Without question, the *écorchés*of 18th-century anatomist Honoré Fragonard are the stars of the show. This small collection of flayed, desiccated, and posed figures of men, human fetuses, and animals serve as the calling card, or the *Mona Lisa*, of the Fragonard Museum of Alfort. But a visit to the museum reveals a far more diverse and compelling collection than Fragonard's work alone.

The museum is on the campus of the National Veterinary School started by Claude Bourgelat in 1765 to improve the healthcare of horses. Fragonard served as its first curator. The modern version of the Musée Fragonard opened in 1903 to display the many pedagogical artifacts of the late 19th and early 20th century. This period saw the rise of scientific research and knowledge but still lacked the modern medicines and practices of today.

Wax and *papier mâché* models and preserved specimens, housed in tall glass display cabinets, illustrate the anatomy and sometimes gruesome maladies of farm animals and pets. Different design methods by wax modelists Richir and Petitcolin reflect distinct ways of coloring anatomy. The lifelike *papier mâché* models of Auzoux, designed to be sold to veterinarians, could be taken apart into individual body parts.

A large room houses the skeletons of horses, cattle, giraffes, and cats and resembles the display of dinosaurs from a paleontology museum. An amusing display of row upon row of horse teeth shows the expected changes over the animal's lifetime. And one wall-sized cabinet houses a magnificent collection of vials with almost 2,000 different parasites, all faithfully catalogued by the museum.

The Fragonard Museum fell into disrepair in the late 20th century, and there was talk of dissolving it and splitting up its collection. But a successful effort restored it to its 1903 appearance and allows you to appreciate how far veterinary science has come.

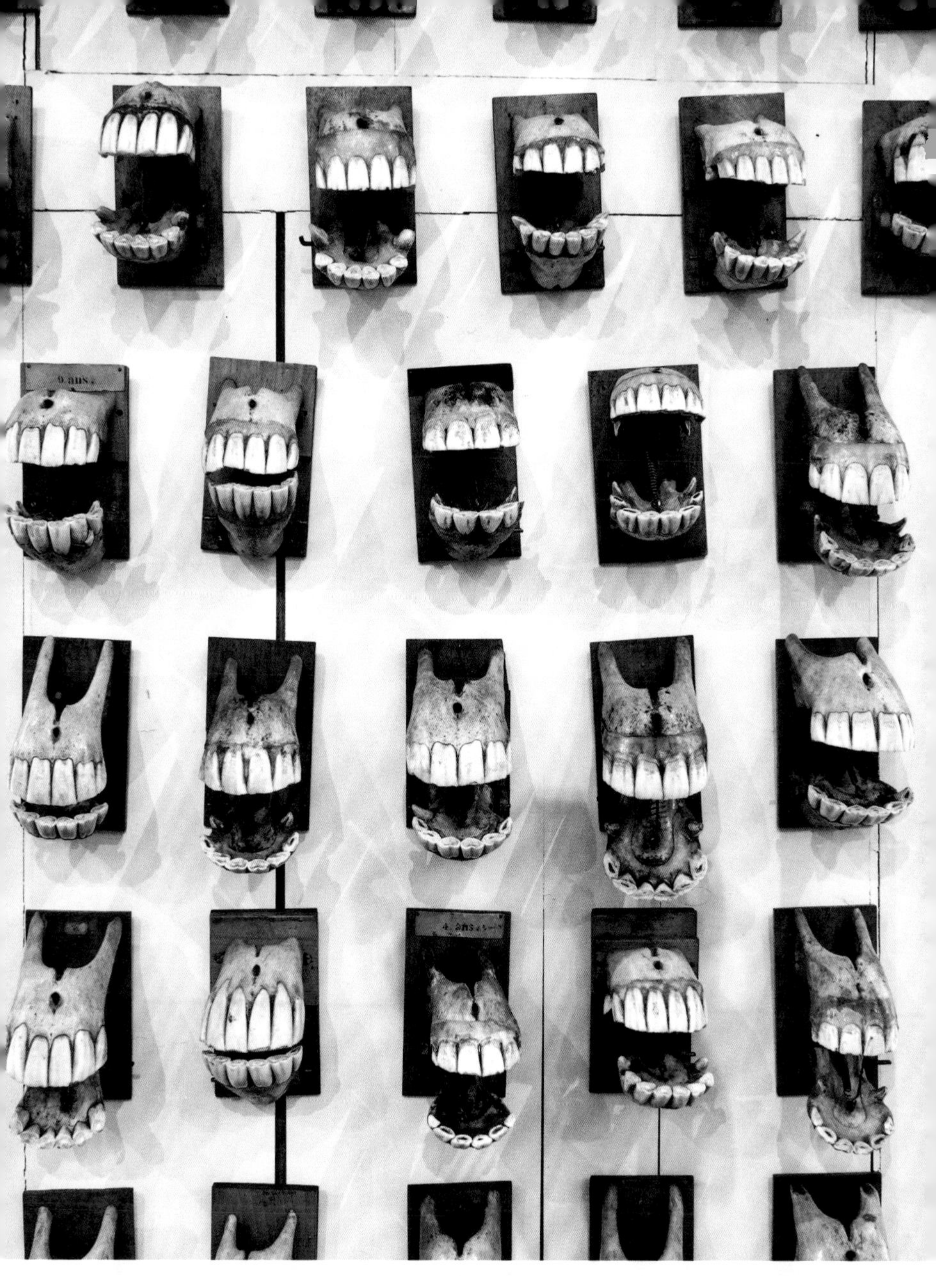

**Address** 7 avenue du Général de Gaulle, 94700 Maisons-Alfort, +33 (0)1 43 96 71 00, www.vet-alfort.fr/domaine-d-alfort/musee-fragonard/infos-pratiques, musee@vet-alfort.fr | **Getting there** Metro to École Vétérinaire de Maisons-Alfort (Line 8); bus 104, 181 to Bouley-École Vétérinaire | **Hours** Daily 9am–5:30pm | **Tip** A botanical garden, also located in the grounds of the National Veterinary School of Alfort, features bee-pollinated, toxic, and medicinal plants.

# 37 Fragonard Perfume Museum

*From civet glands to modern perfumes*

The name of Fragonard Perfumers, established in Grasse in 1926, honors the painter Jean-Honoré Fragonard. The museum was started by former director Jean-François Costa, a passionate collector of perfume vials, *nécessaires*, or travel cases, and other related artifacts.

The museum teaches about the perfume-making process and holds a delightful collection of objects. But why is there a taxidermy civet cat on display? Perhaps you didn't know that the animal's glandular secretions have been added to perfumes for centuries to help smooth and provide warmth to scents. Although largely replaced by synthetics, it's use in perfume is still surprising.

The perfumer's organ resembles the namesake instrument and gave the perfumer ready access to several hundred vials of raw materials. And a tremendous pot still illustrates how techniques for creating perfumes often resemble those for making spirits.

As for Mr. Costa's collection, the earliest treasures from the 3rd millennium B.C. include an Egyptian makeup palette and a makeup bottle from central Asia. There are Grecian amphorae, decorated Roman vials, and a Sicilian bust from the 6th century B.C. A 16th-century vial is composed of rare Venetian glass. An 18th-century artisan produced a crystal bottle with an exquisitely carved ivory case. Marie Antoinette, a well-known perfume lover, is represented by glass and silver bottles in a Moroccan leather case. A First Empire *nécessaire*is filled with sewing and beauty products made of crystal and mother of pearl. A 1930s bottle by René Lalique contained the Fragonard fragrance *Suprême*, while another Lalique bottle holds *Tabac*. And Fragonard's signature scent *Belle de Nuit*filled a gold bottle in a red velvet-lined box.

After immersing yourself in perfume history, you'll emerge into the Fragonard shop, where you'll find an array of fragrant temptations.

Address 9 rue Scribe, 75009 Paris, +33 (0)1 40 06 10 09, musee-parfum-paris.fragonard.com, tourisme@fragonard.com | Getting there Metro to Opéra (Lines 3, 7, 8), Madeleine (Lines 12, 14), Havre-Caumartin (Line 9), Saint-Lazare (Line 13); RER A to Auber, E to Haussmann Saint-Lazare; bus 20, 21, 27, 29, 32, 45, 52, 66, 68, 95 to Opéra | Hours Mon–Sat 9am–5:30pm, Sun 9am–5pm | Tip Around the corner from the museum is the Théatre de l'Athénée Louis-Jouvet, named after the famous French actor and director who died in his dressing room there in 1951 (7 rue Boudreau, www.athenee-theatre.com).

# 38 Freemasonry Museum

*Liberty, equality, conviviality*

One thing you'll learn at the Freemasonry Museum is that there are two main Masonic federations, or *obédiences*, in France. The Grand Orient de France is distinct from the Grande Loge de France and does not follow the Anglo-American tradition, or Scottish Rite. The museum is housed in the same building as the Grand Orient's many ritual temples.

The overall goal of the museum is to teach culture, patrimony, and history. The main gallery itself is a dimly lit space featuring ceiling pin-lights that evoke a starry sky, and a set of tall vitrines filled with over 750 artifacts – banners, statues, watches, and other personal objects among them – belonging to different eras or themes. On one wall, displays explain the lexicon of Freemasonry. You'll learn about the rites and rituals in the lodges and the grades of membership. With Freemasonry having part of its origins among artisans and skilled workers, the grades of Apprentice, Companion, or *Compagnon*, and Master will seem familiar.

On another side of the gallery, a long wooden timeline starts in France around 1725 and continues to the present day. You'll see Freemasonry's run in with Pope Clement XII, its influence in the Second and Third Republics, the various schisms among Freemasons, and its relationship to religion and society. Prominent figures like Jules Ferry, Léon Gambetta, Jules Simon, and Alphonse Mucha were all Masons. Today, the Grand Orient *obédience* counts both men and women among its members and does not require belief in a supreme being.

The museum also focuses on the social aspects of the lodge and the idea of conviviality. The display of an 18th-century white and yellow table service decorated with Masonic symbols highlights the importance of sharing food and friendship. There is always a meal after a meeting of Freemasons, when members can all sit together and enjoy the same food.

Address 16 rue Cadet, 75009 Paris, +33 (0)1 45 23 74 09, www.museefm.org, evenementmuseefm@godf.org | Getting there Metro to Cadet (Line 7), Grands Boulevards (Lines 8, 9); bus 26, 43, 45 to Cadet | Hours Tue–Fri & Sun 10am–12:30pm, 2–6pm, Sat 10am–1pm, 2–7pm | Tip The first lodge of freemasonry in Paris dates to 1725 in Saint-German-des-Près (12 rue de Buci).

# 39__French Playing Card Museum

*Games and divination in Issy*

The town of Issy-les-Moulineaux received a large donation of playing cards from a collector in 1930. Lost in city archives for many years, the collection was rediscovered in the 1980s and became the foundation of the French Playing Card Museum. While playing cards may seem mundane, this museum is anything but that. In fact, this museum was voted "European Museum of the Year" in 1999, a distinction shared with the Guggenheim Museum Bilbao, the Rijksmuseum Amsterdam, and the Design Museum of London, among others.

Housed on two floors, the museum is dimly lit to protect over 11,000 handmade and machine-printed cards from throughout Europe, North America, and Japan and spanning several hundred years. The cards are grouped thematically and temporally and cover games like poker and belote, tarot cards, and divination. Themes can be political, historical, or geographic. Some sets represent the major figures in Victorian England and pre-Revolutionary France, while other sets were designed for learning geography. One set in particular has photographs of 19th-century American West landscapes. Look for the display of cards featuring nudes and a variety of sex positions, hidden demurely behind a red velvet curtain.

Seemingly simple, playing cards can take on so many different forms. Dozens of versions of the Joker card, which appeared originally in the United States in the 1860s and in France by the turn of the 20th century, are displayed on one panel. You can also see how depictions of key tarot cards like Love and Death change over time.

Take note as well of the clever design of the card displays themselves. To maximize space, the French Playing Card Museum has used stacked, sliding, vertical panels that reveal different sets of cards, and wheels that turn 360 degrees to display a complete set of cards on each side.

**Address** 16 rue Auguste Gervais, 92130 Issy-les-Moulineaux, +33 (0)1 41 23 83 60, www.museecarteajouer.com | **Getting there** Metro to Mairie d'Issy (Line 12); RER C to Issy-Val de Seine; tramway to Issy-Val de Seine (Line 2); bus, 169/323, arrêt Musée, TUVIM, arrêt Étienne Dolet | **Hours** Wed–Fri 11am–5pm, Sat & Sun 2–6pm | **Tip** Enjoy expositions about Issy-les-Moulineaux in the Gallery of the History of the City housed in the top floors of the same building and also in the last remaining part of the adjoining 17th-century chateau of the Conti princes.

# 40 Gainsbourg House

*No smoking*

More than a museum, the Gainsbourg House is a window on the world of the great French musician and icon of pop culture. Serge Gainsbourg, whose multiple talents included painting and cinema – not to mention his emblematic look – profoundly marked his time with his disconcerting alter egos, including the famous Gainsbarre of the 1980s.

Brought to life in an audio tour narrated by his daughter Charlotte Gainsbourg, the home, where the spirit of Gainsbourg still feels present three decades after his death, offers an intimate look into the artist's personal and professional life. You'll notice his signature pack of Gitane cigarettes and an ashtray on the coffee table, as if he has just stepped out of the room.

The house is preserved as he left it, full of personal treasures and souvenirs. Look for the little monkeys given to him by his partner Jane Birkin. There are chandeliers in both the kitchen and the bathroom. Explore his office library filled with works by authors he admired, from Huysmans to Rimbaud. You'll see a 19th-century English dentist's chair and a cocktail case he used to entertain fellow singer-songwriter Jacques Dutronc, who donated the "No Smoking" sign placed at the entrance.

The house tour immerses visitors in an environment that is both contemporary and retro. The walls are covered in black fabric and decorated with gold records and photos of Marilyn Monroe. Framed press clippings evoke the *Marseillaise* scandal and add to the place's authenticity. Charlotte's stories are achingly personal.

The adjacent museum provides a timeline of the artist's career, complete with videos, photos, and artifacts. Appropriately, there's a piano bar where you can complete this unforgettable experience with a cocktail. Thanks to Charlotte's commitment, the Maison Gainsbourg has become a living memorial and tribute to one of France's greatest artists.

Address 14 rue de Verneuil, 75007 Paris, www.maisongainsbourg.fr | Getting there Metro to Saint-Germain-des-Prés (Line 4) or Rue du Bac (Line 12); RER C to Musée d'Orsay; Bus 27, 39, 87, 95 to Pont du Carrousel – Quai Voltaire | Hours Tue, Thu, Sat & Sun 10am – 8pm, Wed & Fri 10am – 10:30pm | Tip Madame Arthur is a cabaret located in Montmartre, where both Serge Gainsbourg and his father Joseph Ginsburg played the piano (75 bis Rue des Martyrs, www.madamearthur.fr).

# 41 Gallery of Paleontology & Comparative Anatomy

*Dinosaurs, skeletons, and one still-woolly mammoth*

If the Grande Gallery of Evolution is a modern museum masterpiece, then the Gallery of Paleontology and Comparative Anatomy feels like a wonderful time machine to experience science at the dawn of the 20th century. Inside the ornate building, it's easy to imagine yourself among the visitors at its opening in 1898 viewing the new wonders of modern science. Notably, air conditioning did not yet exist, and even to this day the museum is subject to closure on extremely hot days.

The bottom floor Gallery of Comparative Anatomy is a forest of skeletons that serves to contrast the forms of different species, many of them close cousins. If you read the signage for each specimen, many handwritten in a charming old script, you'll discover incredible origin stories. The skeletons come from all over the world – and also from the zoo on the other side of the Jardin des Plantes. Among them is an ox bought in London that died at the nearby zoo. An African Cape buffalo was donated by the president of the republic. A huge whale was found beached in South Africa. A mummified Apis bull came from ancient Egypt. And an Indian rhinoceros from the royal menagerie of Versailles was killed with a saber during the Revolution.

The upper two floors of the museum are dedicated to paleontology. If you're a real fossil buff, you'll want to examine the extensive collections of ancient marine and plant life on the top floor. But all visitors will want to spend time with the dinosaurs and other creatures from the last ice age. A 35-million-year-old whale and the Durfort mammoth are popular attractions, but don't miss the equally fabulous Siberian mammoth, which was discovered still frozen in 1901 and arrived at the museum in 1912. Not only is its skeleton on exhibit, but also the skin from its head and a still-furry foot. The mammoth's other feet and its organs remain in cold storage.

Address 2 rue Buffon, 75005 Paris, +33 (0)1 40 79 56 01, www.mnhn.fr/fr/galerie-de-paleontologie-et-d-anatomie-comparee, valhuber@mnhn.fr | Getting there Metro to Gare d'Austerlitz (Lines 5, 10), Jussieu (Lines 7, 10); RER C to Gare d'Austerlitz; bus 24, 57, 91 to Gare d'Austerlitz, 63, 89 to Jardin des Plantes | Hours Wed–Mon 10am–6pm | Tip You can buy fossils for your own collection at Carion Mineraux (92 rue St-Louis-en-l'Île, www.carionmineraux.com).

# 42 Galliera Palace Museum

*The history of fashion*

For fashion enthusiasts, the Galliera Palace serves as a sanctuary. Built in the late 19th century, the Beaux Arts-style Galliera Palace is the work of the architect Paul-René-Léon Ginain. The space was designed according to the specifications of Maria Brignole Sale de Ferrari, Duchess of Galliera, who wanted a palace to display her art collection.

Completed in 1894, it was later donated to the City of Paris, and in 1977, it found its purpose as a museum dedicated to fashion. The fashion museum for the City of Paris has been recently renovated and has added new galleries offering visitors a tour of fashion from the 18th century to the present day through regularly renewed exhibits ensuring a fresh perspective and a variety of themes.

This sumptuous collection of more than 250,000 pieces consists of clothing, accessories, posters, drawings, and photographs. In a chronological and thematic journey, you will discover the evolution of fashion through extraordinary pieces that demonstrate the creativity and expertise of couturiers. Extraordinary garments reflect their eras, from 18th-century menswear to avant-garde designs, and from 19th-century corsets to 1950s cocktail dresses. Make sure to look for haute couture from Yves Saint Laurent, Cristobal Balenciaga, Christian Dior, and other icons of design.

Christian Dior's first collection in 1947 marked a turning point in fashion history. His New Look silhouette with rounded shoulders, a defined waist, and full skirts reintroduced an idealized femininity breaking free from the constraints of the wartime period. This event signaled the beginning of a new golden age for haute couture and reinstated Paris as the fashion capital of the world. The Palais Galliera brings to life the entire history of French fashion and elegance spanning several centuries and offering a comprehensive experience for fashion aficionados.

**Address** 10 avenue Pierre 1er de Serbie, 75116 Paris, +33 (0)1 56 52 86 00, www.palaisgalliera.paris.fr | **Getting there** Metro to Iéna or Alma-Marceau (Line 9); RER C to Pont de l'Alma; bus 32, 63, 82 to Iéna, 2, 72, 80, 92 to Alma-Marceau | **Hours** Tue–Sun 10am–6pm | **Tip** Sign up for a walking tour by the Palais Galliera. It will take you through the Yves Saint-Laurent Paris Museum and down Avenue Montaigne, which has famously been home to fashion houses and their studios since the early 20th century (www.ticketterie-parismusees.paris.fr).

# 43 Giacometti Institute

*The artist, the work, and the studio*

The Giacometti Institute, located in the Montparnasse district, holds a remarkable collection of more than 100 sculptures, drawings, prints, and photographs by Alberto Giacometti (1901–1966). The space is human in scale, inviting visitors to connect intimately with the artist's work. Four temporary exhibitions are scheduled each year, ensuring that the viewer can continuously discover new facets of Giacometti's groundbreaking contributions to the art world.

The Institute is set in a private mansion built in 1911 for Paul Follot, a decorator who worked for esteemed clients such as Le Bon Marché. The architecture dates to the transitional period between Art Nouveau and Art Deco. You'll want to notice the remarkable mosaic details in this former studio, which is now a superb showroom for Giacometti's work.

While the artist did not reside here, his nearby studio, referred to as his "studio/cave," at 46 rue Hippolyte Maindron, held great significance. Giacometti spent more than 40 years of his life and created the majority of his oeuvre here. The artist, the work, and the studio were intimately intertwined in this space, where his art came to life. After his death, the studio was returned to its owner.

Annette, the artist's widow, preserved every aspect of the studio, down to the walls, and the institute was able to rebuild it in its entirety. The space is striking for its small size (24 square meters/260 square feet) and its well-used state. You'll see the artist's bed and easels and admire the two *Walking Man* sculptures. Look for busts of his brother and mother, his first sculptures. Giacometti would write his ideas and sketch images directly on the studio's walls, a critical part of his artistic process.

This studio was a mythical place in the Paris of its time, welcoming writers and artists, including Sartre, Genet, and Doisneau. Today, it is a place for enthusiasts of Giacometti's artistic legacy.

**Address** 5 rue Victor Schœlcher 75014 Paris, +33 (0)1 44 54 52 44, www.fondation-giacometti.fr | **Getting there** Metro to Raspail or Denfert-Rochereau (Lines 4, 6); RER B to Denfert-Rochereau; bus 59, 88 to Denfert-Rochereau-Froidevaux, 68 to Victor Considérant | **Hours** Tue–Sun 10am–6pm | **Tip** Take a stroll down Boulevard du Montparnasse past Le Sélect Brasserie, Le Dôme Café, La Coupole Brasserie, and La Closerie des Lilas Restaurant, all lively haunts of Picasso, Vlaminck, Braque, Léger, and Hemingway.

# 44 Grand Gallery of Evolution

*Our impact on the natural world*

Take cover – it's going to be a deluge!

You'll be forgiven for believing it's about to rain inside the Grand Gallery of Evolution, a marvelous example of 19th-century architecture that was transformed into a thoroughly modern museum in the 1990s. In a wonderful light show, this amazing four-story atrium grows dark, followed by thunder and flashes of lightning, and then the sounds of a downpour fills the space. But soon this thunderstorm on the savannah is over, the sun comes out, and all the local animals continue their procession in the bright light of day.

The central message of the Grand Gallery is that diversity results from the evolution of living organisms in a multitude of environments, and it's our duty to preserve them. You'll experience this message through the long history of animals and the work of the naturalists who discovered and described the different classes of species, genetics, and the mechanisms of evolutionary biology.

The museum also emphasizes humans' role and influence over species diversity. We have hunted, domesticated, and otherwise altered animal populations and their development through industrialization, human overpopulation, habitat loss, and resource depletion. Changes to species that used to take eons can now occur within mere decades.

The most cautionary tales of human impact are found in the gallery of endangered and extinct species. Hundreds of taxidermy animals are on display representing species that have gone extinct in recent times or are critically endangered. In France, these species include birds, amphibians, and even brown bears. The bearded vulture is found worldwide but was hunted nearly to extinction in France. A program of reintroduction began in 1978, and as of 2020 there were 47 couples in France. These animals come back to life with the augmented reality experience offered.

**Address** 36 rue Geoffroy Saint-Hilaire, 75005 Paris, +33 (0)1 40 79 56 01, www.mnhn.fr/fr/grande-galerie-de-l-evolution, valhuber@mnhn.fr | **Getting there** Metro to Gare d'Austerlitz (Lines 5, 10), Jussieu (Lines 7, 10); RER C to Gare d'Austerlitz; bus 24, 67, 89 to Buffon-la Mosquée | **Hours** Wed–Mon 10am–6pm | **Tip** Take a short walk to the Paris Mosque and enjoy a meal or a great selection of takeaway pastries at the Moroccan restaurant inside (39 rue Geoffroy Saint-Hilaire, www.la-mosquee.com/le-restaurant).

# 45 Grévin Wax Museum

*Real … or wax?*

The life of a wax figure is hard because wax is so soft. While their bodies are made of resin, their faces are made of wax. So they do get damaged, mostly during vacation season. Every night, the staff repositions the figures, fixes their hair and clothing, and notes any new damage. The process of creating a new wax figure itself is quite extraordinary, requiring up to 15 artisans, several months, and at least two celebrity visits for measurements and facial sculpting. The celebrity might even provide an outfit of their own.

The Grévin Museum, now over 140 years old, is the creation of publisher Arthur Meyer. He solicited the genius of Alfred Grévin, a well-known caricaturist, sculptor, and costumer, to make the museum a reality and lend it his name. The location was once a hotel – look for the "Room #5" sign, chamber doors, and hallways. The museum was combined with a theater, decorated by the sculptor Antoine Bourdelle, that is still used to introduce new wax figures and host events, such as live music performances. But first, you enter the Palais des Mirages, a historic spectacle from the 1900 Universal Exposition and a fantastic display of mirrors, lights, music, and magic.

Of course, you're here to find your favorite celebrities among the approximately 400 wax figures on display throughout the spectacularly ornate spaces. French personalities like Jean-Paul Belmondo, Mimie Mathy, and Kylian Mbappe are joined by Michael Jackson, Shahrukh Khan, and Barack Obama. And it's not just celebrities – there's history, too.

You'll see Louis XIV in his full "Sun King" regalia, General de Gaulle entering Paris, and Joan of Arc tied to the stake. But the museum's most unexpected treasure is the recreation of the 1793 assassination of revolutionary Jean-Paul Marat by Charlotte Corday, which features the actual murder weapon and the bathtub in which he was killed.

Address 10 boulevard Montmartre, 75009 Paris, +33 (0)1 47 70 85 05, www.guimet.fr | Getting there Metro to Grands Boulevards (Lines 8, 9); bus 20, 32, 39 to Grands Boulevards | Hours See website for seasonal hours | Tip Close by, the Saint-Denis Gate was built by Louis XIV on the former site of a fortified gateway of the 14th-century Wall of Charles V. It was the first of four triumphal arches culminating with the Arc de Triomphe (corner of Boulevard de Bonne Nouvelle and Rue Saint-Denis).

# 46 Guimet Museum

*The largest European museum of Asian art*

The National Museum of Asian Arts–Guimet is one of the most exotic cultural places in the capital. Opened in 1889, the Guimet Museum displays an impressive collection representing diverse Asian cultures and civilizations: Southeast Asia, Central Asia, China, Korea, India, Japan, Afghanistan, Pakistan, and the Himalayas. It showcases more than 45,000 objects, the vast majority of which are ancient artworks and archaeological items. This museum is one of the largest in Europe dedicated exclusively to Asian art.

The museum owes its collections to the passion for Asian art of Émile Étienne Guimet, a wealthy industrialist from Lyon and an avid traveler during the late 19th century. An unusual figure, Guimet was initially fascinated by the study of religious history. In 1876, he undertook a trip to the Far East to delve into the study of Buddhism. During his travels, he acquired paintings, Buddhist sculptures, and manuscripts. Upon his return to Paris, inspired by his travels, he made the decision to establish a museum.

In his words, "There are different types of scholars. Those who pull the curtain so as not to be seen and those who make holes in the curtains. Personally, I like to make holes in curtains. I want to see, and I want everyone to see."

With this vision in mind, Guimet commissioned the building of the current museum as a space to exhibit his treasures. They are displayed to convey artistic influences and styles, not only between different periods but equally from one country to another. It is pleasant to stroll through the sleek galleries and soak in the natural light. You can discover the Angkor Buddha, and walk among Khmer statuary, including the bust of Jayavarman VII, whose serenity is captivating, and marvel at warrior armor and porcelain from China and Japan. Opulent and diverse, the works in these collections are quite impressive in both their detail and their grandeur.

Address 6 place d'Iéna, 75016 Paris, +33 (0)1 56 52 54 33, www.guimet.fr, resa@guimet.fr | Getting there Metro to Iéna (Line 9), Trocadéro or Boissière (Line 6); bus 63, 82 to Iéna, 30, 32 to Albert de Mun, 22 to Trocadéro | Hours Wed–Mon 10am–6pm | Tip The Maison Loo, an unusual building sitting in the Plaine Monceau, is a Chinese pagoda that is now home to Pagoda Paris, a private gallery specializing in exhibits and sales of Asian art (48 rue de Courcelles, www.pagodaparis.com).

# 47 Gustave Moreau National Museum

*A house and museum with mysterious works*

The Gustave Moreau National Museum offers an intimate and exclusive experience. The museum invites you to explore the apartment/museum of the renowned Parisian artist Gustave Moreau (1826–1898). This is the only home in Paris to have been transformed into a museum by the artist who lived there. The timeless space features eclectic décor on four levels and an outstanding collection of more than 25,000 pieces, including 15,000 works by Moreau.

In 1852, Louis Moreau acquired a house located in the New Athens district, where Gustave Moreau resided with his parents. After their passing, he decided to have his home/atelier expanded to leave his work to posterity. Vast studios were designed, and a magnificent spiral staircase was installed to connect the two workshops. Since this house/museum opened in 1903, its museography has remained unchanged. Spanning four floors, the museum immerses you in the multifaceted world of the symbolist master. Like his fellow symbolist artists, Moreau sought to embrace the enigmatic nature of his work. Among his notable works, *The Triumph of Alexander the Great* reflects this dreamlike world, filled with mysteries, which Moreau represented throughout his career. This historical painting transforms into a symbolist landscape of a majestic India and pays tribute to the conquerors. Moreau's creative process was driven by meticulous research. He copied Indian architectural motifs and sculptures from Henri Cernuschi's photographic albums. Unconcerned with historical accuracy, he relied on his own documentation to invent a detailed but imaginary India.

Moreau's works are unparalleled; they are imbued with mystery, reflecting the artist's quest to renew the genre of historical painting and deepen its meaning and scope.

Address 14 rue de La Rochefoucauld, 75009 Paris, +33 (0)1 83 62 78 72, www.musee-moreau.fr, info@musee-moreau.fr | Getting there Metro to Trinité-d'Estienne d'Orves or Saint-Georges (Line 12); bus 40, 74 to Saint-Georges, 26, 43 to Trinité | Hours Wed–Mon 10am–6pm | Tip The Verdeau Passage in the Grands Boulevards district was built by its namesake in 1847. Look for antique books, etchings, and other old treasures in this charming passageway (31 bis rue du Faubourg Montmartre).

# 48 History of Immigration Museum

*Creating new lives in France*

The Palais de la Porte Dorée, or Golden Door Palace, is an Art Deco masterpiece on Paris' eastern edge, built for the 1931 Colonial Exposition. The interior murals by painter Pierre Ducos de la Haille reflect the exposition's aim of glorifying France's contributions to the nations it colonized. Today, the Museum of the History of Immigration adopts a much different approach. Reopened in 2023 after renovations, the museum's renewed exhibit space offers visitors a more didactic experience around immigration in France, with an increased focus on recent times and research.

In the stairway leading up to the exhibit spaces are poignant photos of immigrants from different countries, accompanied by evocative words: "Departure," "Passage," "Separation," "Welcome," and "Refuge." The permanent collection is organized chronologically, starting in 1685, when the *Black Code* codified the slave trade, and the *Edict of Fontainebleau* forced the emigration of 100,000 Huguenots. The exhibit highlights the dates of eleven foundational events that tell the story of immigration. Each event is accompanied by personal stories, objects, and media that illustrate immigration's changing nature, primary ethnic groups, and cultural and political impact.

Don't miss poignant stories like Christina Diaz Vergara, a Chilean woman who took refuge in France with her family after the military coup that deposed President Salvador Allende, in 1973. Nikolai Angelov immigrated from Bulgaria and now works on Roma rights and integration. Sit and watch the video of young people, who describe their feelings about being French against the backdrop of their family's origins. Today, more than a quarter of France's population is comprised of immigrants and their descendants, mostly from Europe and the French diaspora.

Address Palais de la Porte Dorée, 293 Avenue Daumesnil, 75012 Paris, +33 (0)1 44 74 85 09, www.histoire-immigration.fr, publics@palais-portedoree.fr | Getting there Metro to Porte Dorée (Line 8); Tramway to Porte Dorée (Line T3a); Bus (46, 201) to Porte Dorée | Hours Tue–Fri 10am–5:30pm, Sat & Sun 10am–7pm | Tip The Square des Anciens-Combattants-d'Indochine was also built for the 1931 exposition and features a cascading fountain and a statue of Athena by Léon-Ernest Drivier (place Édouard-Renard).

# 49 Henri Cartier-Bresson Foundation

*From photojournalism to fine art photography*

The remarkable photographs of Henri Cartier-Bresson (1908–2004), known as the "eye of the century," and photographer Martine Franck (1938–2012), his wife, will take you on a journey back to the origins of photojournalism and fine art photography. The couple established the Henri Cartier-Bresson Foundation to create a community space where they and other contemporary photographers could exhibit their work.

Henri Cartier-Bresson was initially a painter and illustrator before discovering photography by chance, and international media outlets sent him around the world to cover news events. It is said that he "traversed the entirety of the twentieth century," witnessing major historic events, like the liberation of Paris in 1944 and the fall of the Nationalist Party in China in 1949. It seems he was always present at pivotal moments in history. His unique style is clean and luminous, with profound shades of black and white, and he skillfully played with geometry to achieve his compositions. His photos were never cropped.

To fully appreciate Henri Cartier-Besson's work, it is important to understand the way the press covered the news at the time. Back then, publications used a series of photographs to build a story. But instead of covering political moments, Henri Cartier-Besson chose to photograph people and scenes of daily life to tell the story. He would submit unprinted film to his editors, along with punchy and concise notes, and he only saw his own photographs once they were published. His work reveals the intensity of a time in the details captured through his technique and artistry. Exhibitions featuring the work of a contemporary artist with that of either Henri Cartier-Bresson or Martine Franck are curated every three months.

Address 79 rue des Archives, 75003 Paris, +33 (0)1 40 61 50 50, www.henricartierbresson.org | Getting there Metro to Arts et Métiers (Lines 3, 11); bus 75 to Square du Temple | Hours Tue–Sun 11am–7pm | Tip On a drizzly day, grab your camera and a friend, head to the 8th arrondissement, and create your own version of Bresson's 1932 masterpiece, *Behind the Gare Saint-Lazare*.

# 50 History of Medicine

*From amputation to modern surgery*

Anal fistulas were all the rage in the court of Louis XIV. Be grateful that you live in the 21st century.

These are two takeaways from a visit to this spectacular, two-level, wood-paneled hall in the medical school at the University of Paris. The History of Medicine Museum showcases medical and surgical instruments and practices dating back to ancient times.

Instruments are displayed in cases along the walls, while other objects, like anatomical models and furniture, are freestanding in the open hall. The actual instrument used to operate on the Sun King's anal fistula takes pride of place, and you will immediately think that there is no way you would let someone get near you with it. The kit used to perform Napoleon's autopsy is also on display.

The museum is organized chronologically and thematically, so you can see the evolution of equipment and techniques and learn about the people who made significant contributions to medicine. You will find instruments that look familiar, such as speculums and syringes, from as far back as the 16th century. Nonetheless, most early surgical instruments seemed to exist for amputation or trepanation. An 18th-century urology kit is truly frightening. Advances in the understanding of human anatomy in the late 18th century and the development of anesthesia and Pasteur's work in the 19th century revolutionized medicine.

One fascinating example of changing medical practice is eye surgery. You might think that the eye's delicate structure would make it an unlikely candidate for surgery. But medical practice advanced to the point where 19th-century doctors could identify and attempt to treat dozens of distinct eye ailments. More surprisingly, you'll learn that eye surgery is one of the earliest types. Cataract surgery was invented in the 3rd century B.C., and some modern surgical techniques date as far back as 1552.

Address 12 rue de l'ecole de Médecine, 75006 Paris, +33 (0)1 76 53 16 93, u-paris.fr/musee-de-lhistoire-de-la-medecine, musee.histoire-medecine@u-paris.fr | Getting there Metro to Odéon (Lines 4, 10); bus 58, 63, 86, 87, 93 to Saint-Germain-Odéon | Hours Mon–Wed, Fri & Sat 2–5:30pm | Tip The Hotel Dieu is the oldest continuously operating hospital in the world. The current 19th-century building has a beautiful and peaceful courtyard (1 place du Parvis Notre-Dame).

# 51 Hôtel d'Heidelbach

*A Buddhist pantheon*

Located on avenue d'Iéna, the private Heidelbach mansion was built between 1912 and 1915 by the architect René Sergent for the American banker Alfred Samuel Heidelbach and his wife Julie Picard. The neoclassical-inspired building was the private residence of the Heidelbach family and housed their collection of 18th-century European decorative art.

The collection was dispersed after Heidelbach's passing. The mansion was eventually acquired by the Musées de France, and in 1991 it was placed under the purview of the Musée Guimet. During the renovation process, the museum fulfilled Émile Guimet's dream of establishing a Buddhist Pantheon. The majestic space highlights the exquisite beauty of the imperial works on display, and this intimate museum is a worthwhile destination for any art enthusiast.

The first gallery displays works of grand imperial furniture from the Ming and Qin Dynasties. A large imperial wardrobe from the Ming Dynasty sits in the center of the room. It is adorned with intricate lacquer work and embellished with dragons, a symbol of the emperor. The detailed patterns on the wardrobe's façade contrast with the more ethereal garden-themed design adorning its rear.

The second gallery is an ideal setting for two sumptuous Chinese screens. Screens were used to delineate public and private spaces and served to magnify the place of honor. The Qing Dynasty screen (circa 1691) features twelve panels decorated with pine trees and cranes. Exquisite incised detailing on the deep brown lacquer background seamlessly merges with vibrant blue, jade green, gray, and pink hues, creating a mesmerizing visual tableau.

Another room is dedicated to the serene rituals and accoutrements of the tea ceremony. You can experience an authentic tea ceremony for yourself in the garden here, one of the highest forms of the Japanese art of living (by reservation).

**Address** 19 avenue d'Iéna, 75116 Paris, +33 (0)1 56 52 54 33, www.guimet.fr | **Getting there** Metro to Iéna (Line 9), Trocadéro or Boissière (Line 6); bus 63, 82 to Iéna, 30, 32 to Albert de Mun, 22 to Trocadéro | **Hours** Wed–Mon 10–11:30am & 2:30–5:30pm | **Tip** Visit the Pont de l'Alma and seek out the Zouave statue, a French soldier from the Crimean war. During the 1910 flood, this statue emerged as a marker for rising water levels, as its head has never been submerged. Even today, Parisians refer to the Zouave as a measure of the water level in the Seine.

# 52 Hôtel de la Marine

*The 18th century awaits you*

Eager to assert his authority, Louis XV commissioned the construction of his royal square in 1748 in what is now Place de la Concorde. The project was completed in 1774 and included a sculpture of the king and two identical palaces. One of these palaces, the Hôtel de la Marine, served to store the royal furnishings. This is where the king's furniture was produced, cataloged, and restored. The palace also housed administrative offices, restoration workshops, and the apartments of royal civil servants. After the revolution, the Ministry of the Navy had its offices here until 2017.

Now a museum, the palace has rediscovered the sumptuous decor of this mansion from the 18th and 19th century. Twenty or so coats of paint had to be removed to reveal the original colors. Via an audio headset, a guide welcomes you as if you were a friend of the King's steward visiting his apartments and the Navy's ceremonial salons for the very first time.

Each room, from living spaces to bedrooms and bathrooms, is decorated in the sophisticated style of the Age of Enlightenment. You enter through a surprisingly simple lobby – it was customary in the 18th century not to show one's wealth in the first room. The farther one goes into the apartment, the more one will become overwhelmed by its splendor. The King's steward did not hesitate to incorporate opulent furniture from the official inventory, particularly when decorating spaces used by the king himself.

One room, the anteroom, caused a scandal during its time due to its luxury, which was deemed excessive for an ordinary chamber. The large office is decorated with a rare Portor marble fireplace and an exquisite dresser by Jean-Henri Riesener, who served as King Louis XV's cabinetmaker. In the dining room, a large table has been set with opulent dinnerware to simulate the final moments of a meal, as if the King's steward had just stepped away from the table.

Address 2 place de la Concorde, 75008 Paris, +33 (0)1 53 42 87 40, www.hotel-de-la-marine.paris | Getting there Metro to Concorde (Lines 1, 8, 12); bus 42, 45, 52, 72, 73, 84 to Concorde | Hours Sat–Thu 10:30am–7pm, Fri 10:30am–9:30pm | Tip Take a short walk to the Palais Cambon to view its unique architecture and rich heritage, making it a captivating example of the official architecture during the Third Republic (46 rue Cambon).

# 53 Hunting & Nature Museum

*A charming cabinet of curiosities*

Even if you're not a fan of hunting, don't let that deter you from pushing open the doors of this extraordinary and charming museum. From the moment you step inside, you realize that it is unlike any other museum. Instead, it resembles a welcoming home, brimming with wonders and extraordinary artworks. There is something to see in every nook and cranny – the main stairway, lounges, paintings, hunting gear, taxidermy, earthenware, unusual objects, and more. All of this is set in the magnificent mansions of Guénégaud (17th century) and Mongelas (18th century) in the heart of the historic Marais district. This is a truly magical place.

The collections are staged like a fairytale, illustrating the relationship between humans and nature during the 17th and 18th centuries. Here, hunting is presented as an art form. The weapons on display are genuine works of art that were not intended to be used!

Within the museum, you will discover a curiosity cabinet containing peculiarities such as a strange stuffed toy preserved in a jar or even a horned rooster. Don't be surprised when you hear the growls and snarls of an animatronic albino boar's head. The museum contains treasures that arouse curiosity and surprise visitors, encouraging you to question the boundaries between reality and imagination. Its key charm lies in not taking itself too seriously. That's the whole secret here.

The museum staff act as room supervisors, but they will not hesitate to interact with you, pointing out details you might have otherwise missed. The museum also organizes temporary exhibitions of contemporary art that interact surprisingly and beautifully with older works. These exhibitions serve as a reminder that the theme of hunting and contemporary art remains relevant today. It's a museum that is worth discovering and visiting time and again.

**Address** 62 rue des Archives, 75003 Paris, +33 (0)1 53 01 92 40, www.chassenature.org | **Getting there** Metro to Hôtel de Ville (Line 1), Rambuteau (Line 11); bus 29, 75 to Archives-Haudriettes | **Hours** Tue–Sun 11am–6pm | **Tip** Take a well-deserved break at Méert, the legendary pastry shop from Lille. The vanilla waffles are fabulous, and they were General de Gaulle's favorite sweet treat (16 Rue Elzévir, www.meert.fr).

# 54_Jacquemart-André Museum

*A home for collectors*

At the Jacquemart-André Museum, you will discover masterpieces and experience a sumptuous, 19th-century mansion. Inaugurated in 1876, the mansion has stood as a testament to the passion of collectors Édouard André and Nélie Jacquemart. André came from a family of bankers and dedicated his inherited wealth to acquiring an impressive array of artworks. In 1881, he married Jacquemart, an artist. This union was decisive for the creation of the museum, which showcases paintings by Dutch and Flemish masters, as well as 18th-century French and Italian Renaissance artists.

Their style was both eclectic and grandiose and was always designed to best display their art. Édouard André particularly sought French 18th-century works, which were highly coveted at the time. Among the notable acquisitions are works by artists such as Jean Siméon Chardin and Jean-Honoré Fragonard. One painting that warrants special attention is the Élisabeth Vigée-Lebrun's *Portrait of Countess Ekaterina Skavronskaïa* (1790).

Madame Vigée-Lebrun was the official portraitist for Queen Marie-Antoinette. She sought refuge in Naples during the French Revolution. While there, the ambassador for Catherine II of Russia commissioned her to paint a portrait of his wife. Of her subject, Vigée-Lebrun observed, "She is a person of undeniable beauty, but the Countess, as beautiful as an angel, is uneducated and of deplorable conversation." Despite the model's lack of expressive skills, the painting captivates viewers through the delicate brushwork, the vibrant chromaticism of the fabrics, and the elegant pose exuding a dreamy charm.

The Flemish and Dutch collection here is equally admirable, featuring works by Van Dyck and Rembrandt. The couple also amassed a veritable museum of Italian art from the Quattrocento period (1400–1499).

Address 158 boulevard Haussmann, 75008 Paris, +33 (0)1 45 62 11 59, www.musee-jacquemart-andre.com | Getting there Metro to Miromesnil (Lines 9, 13); RER A to Charles de Gaulle-Étoile; bus 22, 43, 52 to Haussmann-Courcelles | Hours Daily 10am–6pm | Tip Founded in 1840, the Librairie Auguste Blaizot is one of the most famous bookstores in France. It specializes in bookbinding and features decor typical of the 1930s (164 rue du Faubourg Saint-Honoré, www.librairieblaizot.fr).

# 55 Jean Dubuffet Foundation

*Unfettered imagination*

The Jean Dubuffet Foundation stands as one of the first foundations ever established by an artist. The foundation was created in 1974, soon after Jean Dubuffet (1901–1985) had completed the Closerie Falbala, a monumental sculpture listed as a historical monument. At this late stage in the artist's career, Dubuffet desired to present his works as a cohesive whole, believing that a comprehensive view of an artist's body of work is necessary to understand their artistic vision truly. Motivated by this vision, he decided to establish an independent foundation around his body of work.

He continued to create many works until his passing and donated the paintings to the foundation. Today, the foundation holds more than 2,500 of the artist's paintings, sculptures, architectural models, gouaches, drawings, and prints. The collections are assembled in Perrigny-sur-Yerres, and exhibitions are held here in the Paris home Dubuffet acquired in 1962.

The foundation organizes two temporary exhibits per year of works by Jean Dubuffet exploring various themes. They showcase the multifaceted nature of his art. He is one of the most famous and also the most controversial European artists of the post-war period. Dubuffet possessed an unbounded imagination, reflected in his diverse work that included paintings, assemblages, drawings, and sculptures that oscillate between abstraction and childlike figuration.

Dubuffet relentlessly questioned the conventions of Western art and culture of his time. His anti-culture positions drove him to constantly invent new materials and art forms. He championed self-taught artists and became a pioneer of Art Brut, a term he coined to refer to "works executed by people untouched by traditional artistic culture" and unaware that they were producing art. All of Dubuffet's artworks reflect his rejection of academic painting and his quest to redefine the limits of art.

Address 137 rue de Sèvres, 75006 Paris, +33 (0)1 47 34 12 63, www.fondationdubuffet.com, contact@fondationdubuffet.com | Getting there Metro to Duroc (Lines 10, 13); bus 82, 92 to Duroc | Hours Mon–Fri 2–6pm | Tip A trip to Périgny-sur-Yerres, just outside Paris, is essential for Dubuffet devotees. You will discover his models, paintings, and sculptures, including the Closerie Falbala (7 bis Sentier des Vaux, Périgny).

# 56 Jean-Jacques Henner National Museum

*History of a mansion and a painter*

The Jean-Jacques Henner National Museum is located in a mansion in the heart of Plaine Monceau in the 17th arrondissement, a rare example of private architecture under the Third Republic. The district was popular among artists in the late 19th century. The painter Guillaume Dubufe (1853–1909), a social figure in the Plaine Monceau scene, made the mansion his home and studio. It was acquired in 1921 by Marie Henner, the niece of the painter Jean-Jacques Henner (1829–1905). In 1923, it was transformed into a national museum dedicated to the artist, showcasing both his work and the history of the house.

During the 1870s, the Plaine Monceau district was fashionable and attracted artists and socialites. The actress Sarah Bernhardt started the trend when she moved here, followed by celebrities such as Alexandre Dumas fils and Edmond Rostand. The mansion, which has been restored in its entirety, reflects the eclectic aesthetic of its time. The mix of styles is taken to the extreme: Neo-Gothic, neo-Renaissance, and Japanism are mixed in the fashion of its time.

You will explore the career of Jean-Jacques Henner, from his humble beginnings in Alsace to his triumphs in Paris. Coming from a peasant background, he was initially discovered for his drawings. He then entered the Beaux-Arts School and received the prestigious Prix de Rome, which would launch a celebrated career. Jean-Jacques Henner is not affiliated with any particular school; he defies categorization. Nourished by many influences, he painted a wide variety of subjects, including landscapes, portraits, nymphs, and nudes, employing several styles from academic to idealized works. His ethereal redheaded women played a significant role in the artist's fame. Henner is a painter who deserves to be rediscovered.

Address 43 avenue de Villiers, 75017 Paris, +33 (0)1 83 62 56 17, www.musee-henner.fr, publics@musee-henner.fr | Getting there Metro to Monceau (Line 2), Malesherbes (Line 3); RER C to Pereire; bus 20, 93 to Place du Général Catroux | Hours Tue & Fri 2–8:30pm, Wed & Thu 2–7pm, Sat 11:30am–7pm | Tip The museum organizes walking tours in the Plaine Monceau district focused on a variety of themes (www.musee-henner.fr/type-evenement/visite).

# 57 Jérôme Seydoux-Pathé Foundation

*A journey through early filmmaking*

When you record a 4K home video on your smartphone, it feels like a miraculous use of modern technology. That is, until you visit the Jérôme Seydoux-Pathé Foundation. The foundation's permanent exhibit of cameras and projectors produced by the Pathé company in the first half of the 20th century will remind you that, although the equipment has improved vastly, the roots of personal moviemaking go back over a hundred years.

The Pathé brothers – Charles, Émile, Théophile, and Jacques – were early pioneers of music and movies. The foundation's collection of 150 machines traces over 50 years of innovation, starting with their phonographs of the late 19th century. The Pathé company turned to movie equipment and filmmaking starting in 1896 with a focus on bringing the art of making movies to the public. The 1910s and 1920s were a period of tremendous innovation at the company, and the 1930s onward focused on making equipment ever more accessible to amateurs.

The collection includes many iconic machines, such as the 1896 35mm Cinématographe-type Lumière, the 9.5mm 1922 Pathé-Baby, the 1924 Cocorico, and the more modern post-war Joinville and Webo models. Be sure to crank the handle of the early film projector to get a real sense of how they operated. Each generation of camera equipment was more capable and more portable. Like modern printers cartridges, the chief money-maker for Pathé was the film used in its cameras.

The foundation pays homage to film and Pathé in an incredible venue. The thoroughly modern building by Renzo Piano has a cinema façade attributed to Auguste Rodin. Early silent films are presented in its theater, accompanied by piano students from the National Conservatory of Music. Saturday tours provide visitors with the opportunity to get close to the curved glass ceilings.

Address 73 avenue des Gobelins, 75013 Paris, +33 (0)1 83 79 18 96, fondation-jeromeseydoux-pathe.com, contact@fondationpathe.com | Getting there Metro to Place d'Italie (Lines 5, 6), Les Gobelins (Line 7); bus 27, 47, 59, 83 to Banquier | Hours Tue & Fri 2–8:30pm, Wed & Thu 2–7pm, Sat 11:30am–7pm | Tip Take the backstage Rex Studios tour at the iconic 1932 Art Deco movie palace Le Grand Rex (1 boulevard Poissonière, www.legrandrex.com).

# 58 Jeu de Paume

*Images in their broadest sense*

Inaugurated in 1862, the Jeu de Paume building was a Parisian venue dedicated to this sport, the precursor to court tennis. In the early 20th century, it underwent a transformation and became an exhibition gallery. During World War II, it was used as a storage and transit space for works of art looted by the Nazi regime. After the war, it found a new purpose as the Impressionist Museum. It was only in 2004 that the museum, also named Jeu de Paume, became an art center dedicated to 20th and 21st century images in the broadest sense of the term: photography, video, multimedia contemporary art, cinema, and digital creations.

The primary objective of Jeu de Paume is to provide a space for temporary exhibitions of photography and related arts by centralizing photographic archives scattered throughout various French museums. Jeu de Paume showcases the work of recognized, lesser known, and emerging artists interested in juxtaposing different historical or contemporary narratives. You can explore monographic exhibitions featuring established artists like Cindy Sherman, William Kentridge, and Philippe Halsman alongside new talents such as Omer Fast and Oscar Muñoz. Group exhibitions highlight contemporary issues, such as, "The Image Supermarket" (2020), which raises the problem of the overproduction of images in today's society.

The museum is constantly exploring new methods and new media, exemplified by expanding its reach through *Palm*, a magazine published by Jeu de Paume, and the creation of a website dedicated to online artistic creation, where programming includes artist projects and thematic exhibitions curated by digital art specialists. It also hosts thematic film cycles, symposiums, seminars, and educational activities. Through these diverse initiatives Jeu de Paume seeks to encourage the public to reflect on the role of images in art and society.

**Address** 1 place de la Concorde, 75001 Paris, +33 (0)1 47 03 12 50, www.jeudepaume.org, accueil@jeudepaume.org | **Getting there** Metro to Concorde (Lines 1, 8, 12); bus 42, 45, 52, 72, 73, 84 to Concorde | **Hours** Fri–Mon & Wed 11am–7pm, Thu 11am–9pm | **Tip** Enjoy a walk on the grounds of the Palais Royal, where you'll meander past the garden, the Comédie Française, the theater of the Palais-Royal, shops, and the Colonnes de Buren.

# 59 Lafayette Anticipations

*Where works of art are both produced and exhibited*

Lafayette Anticipations, the corporate foundation of the Galeries Lafayette, opened to the public in 2018 in a 19th-century industrial building in the heart of the Marais district. It is the brainchild of Galeries Lafayette's chairman Nicolas Houzé, a major collector of contemporary art. The space was designed as a "curatorial machine," with a steel and glass exhibition tower set in its central courtyard.

The foundation's project is designed around producing artworks and supporting artists through production assistance. It aims to engage visitors in witnessing the latest artistic trends. The foundation is committed to free admission. The idea behind the space in a former industrial building was to provide a production site in the basement. Here, artists have access to a fleet of machines that can help them produce a wide variety of works using a diverse array of materials and complex techniques. The architect Rem Koolhaas has leveraged the inner courtyard to gain space by turning it into a mobile exhibition tower with 49 possible configurations. Artists can take advantage of this tool and imagine a scenography with all its possibilities. They can produce their works in the studio and then exhibit them at the foundation. On weekends, the studio is open to visitors.

Contemporary art can be perplexing, and so the foundation has set up a team of docents, who are stationed at every level of the exhibition space. The team is made up of art history students, designers, artists, and they each have their own perspectives. They are not there to deliver scholarly interpretations but to start a dialogue and exchanges with visitors. There are temporary exhibitions each year, as well as festivals of contemporary music, dance, and theater between each exhibition. Lafayette Anticipations is a place where you'll want to return and continue reflecting on artistic movements.

Address 9 rue du Plâtre, 75004 Paris, +33 (0)1 42 74 95 59, www.lafayetteanticipations.com, contact@lafayetteanticipations.com | Getting there Metro to Rambuteau (Line 11), Hôtel de Ville (Lines 1, 11); bus 29, 75 to Archives-Rambuteau, 67, 69, 76, 96 to Hôtel de Ville | Hours Fri–Mon & Wed 11am–7pm, Thu 11am–9pm | Tip Medieval houses are exceedingly rare in Paris. You can discover two 16th-century timber houses nearby at 11 rue François Miron.

# 60 Le Corbusier Foundation

*Maison La Roche: another vision of architecture*

The Le Corbusier Foundation is a place of pilgrimage for architecture enthusiasts. The site encompasses two interconnected residences known as the Laroche House and the Jeanneret House. These buildings showcase the groundbreaking and radical ideas of Le Corbusier (1887–1965). Architect, urban planner, painter, theorist, and a major figure of 20th-century architecture, Le Corbusier is one of the principal figures of Modernism.

The villas look simple and white from the outside. Built in 1923 and 1925 by Le Corbusier and Pierre Jeanneret, his partner and cousin, these houses are part of the purist villa series. The designs adhere to a functionalist approach. The interior of the Maison Laroche shows off Le Corbusier's disciplined attention to detail and rigorous principles. This construction marks the initial exploration of his "five points of a new architecture": pilotis (columns), the roof garden, the free plan, the horizontal window, and the free façade. In Le Corbusier's work, color is used to accentuate the architecture. He stated, "The interior of a house must be white, but in order for white to be appreciated, there must be the presence of a well-regulated polychromy."

Within these walls, you can immerse yourself in Le Corbusier's world of colors. Devoting himself to daily painting in his house-studio, he arranged colors like a pictorial composition. Le Corbusier combines light ultramarine blue with burnt sienna or contrasts dark gray with light red ochre, and even dares to juxtapose them with ultramarine blue. All of a sudden, an apparently ordinary wall becomes a masterpiece of composition. Even the radiators have not escaped his discerning eye, as they are covered in anthracite or a light-blue gray that contrasts with the wall against which they rest. Today, Le Corbusier's work is still startling, and a visit here is a wonderful lesson in architecture.

Address 55 rue du Docteur Blanche, 75016 Paris, +33 (0)1 42 88 75 72, www.fondationlecorbusier.fr, reservation@fondationlecorbusier.fr | Getting there Metro to Jasmin (Line 9), Michel-Ange Auteuil (Lines 9, 10); bus 52 to Mozart, PC1 to Suchet-Raffet | Hours Tue–Sat 10am–6pm | Tip Don't miss Le Corbusier's apartment/studio on 24 rue Nungesser-et-Coli, also in the 16th arrondissement. He lived in this apartment with his wife Yvonne Gallis (1930–1957) from 1934 until his death in 1965.

# 61_Legion of Honor Museum

*Tributes to France's foremost yet lost woman painter*

The Legion of Honor and the Orders of Chivalry Museum, in the opulent Hôtel de Salm, is a place of history, tradition, and bling. Several thousand French citizens receive this honor each year, and the origins of such medals in France go back as far as the 12th century.

The Legion of Honor itself was created by Napoleon Bonaparte in 1802, and many different types of medals have been awarded, some for valor in war and others for achievements in arts and industry. The museum displays medals awarded throughout history both by France and other countries. A display about Valéry Giscard d'Estaing includes many medals he received from foreign governments.

A notable recipient of the Legion of Honor, with displays dedicated to her many medals, is the 19th-century French painter Rosa Bonheur. One of the most famous and well-paid artists of her day, Bonheur was an accomplished painter of animals and a friend to many famous personalities, including the American showman Buffalo Bill. She was the first woman artist to receive the Legion of Honor. Her medal was presented to her by Empress Eugenie in 1865, and in 1894 she was promoted from the rank of Knight to Officer. She always wore the small rosette that identified her as an honoree, and you can see it on the robes on display at her home in Thomery.

In addition to Bonheur's medal from the Legion of Honor, the museum displays several other medals that she received during her lifetime. In 1865, she received the cross of Saint Charles from Emperor Maximilian of Mexico. This was followed by the Order of Isabelle the Catholic (Spain) in 1880, the Order of Léopold (Belgium) in 1885, and the Cross of Merit in the Arts and Sciences from the Duchy of Saxe-Cobourg-Gotha in 1892. She was both a Knight and an Officer of the Portuguese Order of Saint James of the Sword. Despite these great honors, Bonheur largely disappeared from history until the 2022 exhibition of her work at the Orsay Museum.

**Address** 2 rue de la Légion d'honneur, 75007 Paris, +33 (0)1 40 62 84 25, www.legiondhonneur.fr | **Getting there** Metro to Solférino (Line 12); RER C to Musée d'Orsay; bus 68, 69, 73, 87 to Musée d'Orsay | **Hours** Wed–Sun 1–6pm | **Tip** Venture an hour outside Paris to visit the chateau-museum of Rosa Bonheur (12 rue Rosa Bonheur, 77810 By-Thomery, www.chateau-rosa-bonheur.fr).

# 62 Louis Vuitton Foundation

*A hotspot for culture and art*

An iconic presence in the French cultural landscape, the Louis Vuitton Foundation made its mark on the edge of the Bois de Boulogne in 2014. The building, a futuristic sailboat resting on a mirror of water and designed by the architect Frank Gehry, was commissioned by Bernard Arnault, CEO of the LVMH Group and an avid collector of contemporary art. This building alone is worth the visit. Head to the rooftop patios to enjoy views of the Bois de Boulogne, Paris, and La Défense.

The foundation houses a collection of artworks from 1960 to the present day. Some of these works engage in a dialogue with the architecture of the building. As you wander through the corridors near the pool, you will encounter mirrors created by artist Olafur Eliasson, playing with light and color. From various vantage points, both inside and outside the colonnade, multiple perspectives converge, echoing the waves suggested by the building's design. The interplay of mirrors can be an interactive experience, inviting visitors to engage with the living architecture.

The permanent collection, unveiled through a series of events, is built upon its founder's affirmed and desired artistic positions. It is organized around four lines: contemplative, pop, expressionist, music/sound. You can explore works by renowned artists such as Andy Warhol, Jean-Michel Basquiat, Gerhard Richter, Ellsworth Kelly, and Thomas Schütte.

In addition, the foundation organizes two temporary exhibitions every year. These often blockbuster events showcase modern and contemporary art. Past exhibitions have included "The Chtchoukine Collection" and "The New World of Charlotte Perriand." The foundation supports emerging artists through the Open Space Program, offering them carte blanche to showcase their creativity each year. It also hosts concerts and recitals, inviting choreographers from all over the world.

Address 8 avenue du Mahatma Gandhi, 75116 Paris, +33 (0)1 40 69 96 00, www.fondationlouisvuitton.fr, contact@fondationlouisvuitton.fr | Getting there Metro to Les Sablons (Line 1); bus 73 to La Garenne-Colombes-Charlebourg | Hours See website for hours and events | Tip Ride all the rides at the Jardin d'Acclimatation, Paris' only amusement park, in the Bois de Boulogne (www.jardin d'acclimatation.fr).

# 63 Louvre Museum

*A private journey*

Once inside the Louvre Museum, you will be struck by its vibrant atmosphere and grandeur. The Louvre is the largest and most visited museum in the world, with over 14 kilometers (9 miles) of gallery space and 38,000 works of art. Unfortunately, some pieces in the museum steal the show, obscuring many collections that make the Louvre such an astonishingly rich venue.

So avoid the crowds and venture into the Richelieu Wing to find a treasure trove of marvels and awe-inspiring spaces that will take you from a king's retreat to the opulent apartments of Napoleon III, with a detour to the ancient cities of Mesopotamia.

The journey begins in the light-filled Marly Court. The Château de Marly served as King Louis XIV's summer residence. Although the château and its grounds fell victim to the ravages of the French Revolution in 1789 and were ultimately destroyed in 1795, some of the park's statues of ancient mythological divinities have survived. Visitors can admire them, as well as Antoine Coysevox's breathtaking horse sculptures. Moving forward, you will go back in time to 2340 B.C. with the captivating statue of Nu-banda Ebih-Il. With its blue lapis lazuli eyes, this figure was an influential personality who worked in the ancient city-state of Mari in modern Syria.

The next stop brings you face-to-face with the 1792–1750 B.C. Code of Hammurabi, the oldest known legal text. Hammurabi, the king of Babylon, had a set of laws engraved on stone slabs and distributed throughout his kingdom. Stepping into the Khorsabad courtyard, you are transported to the 8th century B.C. at the heart of the Assyrian Empire. Here, imposing winged bulls with human heads serving as protective genies guard the entrance to the palace of Sargon II.

The tour ends in the splendor of the 19th century with a visit to the apartments of Napoleon III which boasts opulent spaces that reflect the era's taste for luxury and comfort.

Address 99 rue de Rivoli, 75001 Paris, +33 (0)1 40 20 53 17, www.louvre.fr, info@louvre.fr | Getting there Metro to Palais Royal-Musée du Louvre (Lines 1, 7); bus 27, 39, 68, 95 to Musée du Louvre, 21, 69, 72 to Palais Royal-Musee du Louvre | Hours Mon, Wed, Thu 9am–6pm, Fri 9am–9:45pm, Sat & Sun 9am–6pm | Tip Just a stone's throw from the Louvre is the Galerie Vérot-Dodat, one of the few covered passageways in the district and the place to find sophisticated shops (19 rue Jean-Jacques Rousseau).

# 64 Luxembourg Museum

*Art from a different angle*

The exhibitions held at the Luxembourg Museum are truly a highlight of Parisian cultural life. The museum is steeped in history. It has been a force of cultural influence in France for more than two centuries. Inaugurated in 1750, it was the first museum of ancient art open to the public. In 1818, Louis XVIII approved the establishment of a museum dedicated to living artists in the Palais du Luxembourg. It served as an official center for art dissemination; the best works were transferred to the Louvre after the artists' deaths. While this museum doesn't have a permanent collection, its main focus is on organizing ambitious temporary exhibitions.

The museum showcases exhibitions exploring paintings, photography, or decorative arts, always with a captivating focus, such as the recent "Peintres Femmes, 1780–1830: Birth of a Struggle." At last, here is a museum that gives women their due. It is no longer controversial to say that women's artwork lacks visibility and that their role in history – written by men – has been overlooked. This exhibit revealed how women painted women, reclaiming their own representation, rather than the way male artists portrayed them. It shed light on the struggle women faced to gain recognition and acceptance in the world of fine art.

Another exhibition, "Pionnières: Artists in the Paris of the Roaring Twenties," highlighted the role played by women in shaping major artistic movements of the modern era. These pioneering women, such as Tamara de Lempicka, Sonia Delaunay, and Chana Orloff, were born at the turn of the 20th century and gained access to art schools that had been the domain of men. They were the first to be acknowledged as artists in their own right and brought forth new, distinctively feminine approaches to art. This museum's diverse array of compelling subjects and themes attracts crowds of enthusiastic visitors.

Address 19 rue de Vaugirard, 75006 Paris, +33 (0)1 40 13 62 00, museeduluxembourg.fr | Getting there Métro to Saint Sulpice (Line 4), Mabillon (Line 10), Rennes (Line 12); RER B to Luxembourg; bus 58, 84, 89 to Musée du Luxembourg, 63, 70, 86, 96 to Église Saint Sulpice | Hours Mon 10:30am–10pm, Tue–Sun 10:30am–7pm, closed between exhibitions | Tip In 1630, Marie de Medici commissioned Florentine engineer Thomas Francine to create the wondrous, recently renovated Medici Fountain in the Luxembourg Garden.

# 65_Magic Museum

*These illusions are for real*

A basement in the historic Marais district has been transformed into a magical place. Within its 16th-century stone vaults, the Magic Museum and the accompanying Museum of Automatons are designed to delight and surprise both children and adults. Children will love the live magic performances and the wall of carnival mirrors.Everybody loves a good magic trick, and who doesn't like to see themselves altered into hilarious and unexpected shapes?

The museum is both a collection of artifacts and a review of great French and international magicians. Learn about the contributions of major magicians and the objects and stories associated with them. You'll see the first model of the cabinet that American magician Howard Thurston used in his "Sawn Women" illusion, the Egyptian sarcophagus from Dicksonn's disappearing act, and the pistol for French magician Jean-Eugène Robert-Houdin's "The Invulnerable Magician." Spoiler alert: The exhibit reveals the secret to catching bullets with your teeth.

Did you know that the escape artist Harry Houdini took his stage name from Robert Houdin? Were you aware that pioneering filmmaker Georges Méliès started his career as a magician? One of his first films showed him doing a conjuring trick.

The second part of the museum houses a different type of magic. In addition to the fortune teller booth and Marvo the Mystic, the interactive Museum of Automatons contains over 100 examples of mechanical objects or scenes that come alive at the touch of a button. Watch a bar brawl, a military parade, a grinder sharpening his knives, an animated Eiffel Tower, or Mickey Mouse. See dancing ladies or a blue elephant saving itself from a dreaded mouse. Finish your tour with the life-sized animatronic figures. It's a huge endeavor to keep all the automatons running, so take your time. Each one is in some way whimsical, amusing, or shocking.

**Address** 11 rue Saint-Paul, 75004 Paris, +33 (0)1 42 72 13 26, www.museedelamagie.com, contact@museedelamagie.com | **Getting there** Metro to Saint-Paul (Line 1); bus 69, 76, 96 to Saint-Paul | **Hours** Wed, Sat & Sun 2–7pm | **Tip** The unique café/dinner theater Le Double Fond offers magic with your aperitif (1 place du Marché Sainte-Catherine, www.doublefond.com).

# 66 Maillol Museum

*The artist who loved women*

The Maillol Museum was inaugurated in 1995 in an 18th-century mansion, its façade embellished with a famous fountain by Edmé Bouchardon, *Fontaine aux Quatre Saisons*. Best known to Parisians for its temporary exhibitions, this museum is home to the largest collection of works by Aristide Maillol (1861–1944), an artist who reinvented modern sculpture during his time. The museum owes its existence to Dina Vierny, Maillol's muse, who established her foundation to promote his artistic legacy. In addition to sculptures, the museum provides an overview of Maillol's artistic range, encompassing paintings, drawings, terracottas, and tapestries. Watch the schedule for two to three temporary exhibitions per year on various artistic trends from the 20th and the 21st centuries.

Best known for his majestic sculptures of nude women, Maillol came to the discipline late in life. He began his artistic journey as a painter before venturing into tapestry and decorative arts. Around 1895, he started exploring sculptures by initially crafting small-scale, wooden figures. During his early career, Maillol was closely associated with artists such as Pierre Puvis de Chavannes and the Nabis, including Maurice Denis. He was also Auguste Rodin's contemporary.

Maillol's fascination with the female figure is palpable throughout his work. His drawings of Dina Verny, often serving as preparatory sketches for his sculptures, allow us to understand the genesis of his statues. His sculptures portray sensual bodies characterized by rounded and smooth contours and well-defined anatomical structures, realized through simple geometric forms. Maillol eschewed any form of art that opposed Rodin's expressionism. He sought purity infused with measured sensuality. Maillol stands among the sculptors who propelled statuary into the modern age, employing the figure as means to reach a pure form.

Address 59-61 rue de Grenelle, 75007 Paris, +33 (0)1 42 22 62 28, www.museemaillol.com, contact@museemaillol.com | Getting there Metro to Saint Sulpice (Line 4), Sèvres Babylone (Line 10), rue du Bac (Line 12); bus 68, 84 to Charlotte Picrrand, 63, 83, 94 to Varenne-Raspail | Hours Wed 10:30am–10pm, Thu–Tue 10:30am–6:30pm | Tip Several Maillol statues of female nudes, donated to the French state by Dina Vierny, truly come alive in the Tuileries Garden near the Triumphal Arch of the Carrousel.

# 67 Mariage Frères Tea Museum

*All things tea*

Since 1854, Mariage Frères has sold some of the finest tea in the world. Starting in 1983, the company opened shops throughout Paris. In addition to the collection of huge canisters of different tea expertly offered by the knowledgeable, white-coated staff of tea sommeliers at all its locations, three stores also have tea salons and museums. The museums make a welcome addition to a day exploring the world of tea and sampling a pot of the perfect brew.

If you were a tea buyer, a traveler in search of adventure and fortune, or simply someone who took their tea very seriously, you might have collected the objects in the museum on rue du Bourg-Tibourg. The history of tea and the tea trade is on display. Tea leaves were originally transported in bamboo baskets or earthenware jars, which were later replaced by boxes. Common varieties were packed in paper-lined bamboo crates, while high quality teas were packed in decorated lacquered chests. The smallest chests were reserved for the finest teas.

The first domestic tea containers were the jars that arrived from China. Later, Europeans began to manufacture boxes in a variety of shapes and sizes. Mariage Frères' collection includes designs made in lacquer, metal, and porcelain. As you might expect, the extensive display of teapots and teacups is as varied as the boxes and tins.

Look for two charming objects in particular. A beautiful wicker basket with a full tea service, including a silver teapot, tea tins, porcelain cups, and saucers, evokes afternoon tea *en plein air*. A velvet lined salesman's case holds the sample tins for six different varieties of Lapsang Souchong and bears the assurance, "Imported directly from China."

Back downstairs in the tea shop, you can purchase a treasure of your own. Perhaps a solid silver reproduction of a teapot from London's Victoria and Albert Museum in the shape of a resting camel?

Address 30 rue du Bourg-Tibourg, 75004 Paris, +33 (0)1 42 72 28 11, www.mariagefreres. com/FR/musee_du_the.html, info@mariagefreres.com | Getting there Metro to Hôtel de Ville (Lines 1, 11); bus 67, 72 to Rue Vieille du Temple-Mairie du 4ème | Hours Daily 10:30am – 7:30pm | Tip Another small tea museum is located within the Saint-Germain-des-Prés outpost of Mariage Frères (13 rue des Grands Augustins).

# 68 Marmottan Monet Museum

*Home of the great Impressionists*

It is most likely that you're visiting the Marmottan Monet Museum to see the largest collection of Monet paintings – and with good reason. Victorine Donop de Monchy donated *Impression, Sunrise*in the 1940s, followed by Michel Monet's donation of over 100 of his father's paintings in 1966. From spring until fall, follow your visit to the museum with Monet's house in Giverny and its famous lilypond.

But the museum is much more than just Monet. Paul Marmottan, a specialist in the Empire period, inherited a mansion in Passy in 1883, expanded it and designed its décor, and combined his father's collection of medieval and Renaissance art with his own 18th and early 19th century acquisitions, including Napoleon's bed. Marmottan's collection remains an important part of the museum.

Among the museum's other famous Impressionists is Berthe Morisot. With 25 paintings, 50 drawings, sketchbooks, and correspondence, the museum holds the largest collection of her work. She was a full member of the group of French Impressionists that included Monet, Cézanne, Degas, and Renoir. She was related to Manet through marriage. While she was admitted to the official Salon in 1864, she later joined the Impressionists in most of their exhibitions.

Morisot worked and exhibited successfully in several media, including watercolors for which she was particularly known, plus pastels, drawings, and oils. Her work is characterized by vibrant colors and a very light touch as she painted the people and places around her. Frequent subjects were women, children such as her daughter Julie, and landscapes like those in the nearby Bois de Boulogne. In her later years, Morisot's final paintings were often preceded by several preparatory form and color studies. This is particularly true of the spectacular *Le Cerisier*, which serves as the centerpiece of the gallery dedicated solely to her.

Address 2 Rue Louis-Boilly, 75016 Paris, +33 (0)1 44 96 50 33, www.marmottan.fr | Getting there Metro to La Muette (Line 9); RER C to Boulainvilliers; bus 32, 70 to Louis Boilly | Hours Fri–Sun, Tue & Wed 10am–6pm, Thu 10am–9pm | Tip La Petite Ceinture du 16ème is a pleasant greenway running from the Jardin du Ranelagh to Porte d'Auteuil on the site of the former 19th-century circular railway (www. paris.fr/equipements/petite-ceinture-du-16e-pc-16-16227).

# 69 Méliès Museum

*The origins of film at La Cinémathèque Française*

La Cinematheque Française, with its incredible library, comprehensive film series, and rich expositions, is the center of everything movie and filmmaking in France. It is fitting that the museum is dedicated to the life and work of Georges Méliès, the grandfather of cinema and a hero to generations of filmmakers, set designers, and special effects houses.

Those whose first exposure to Méliès was the Martin Scorsese movie *Hugo*will be surprised to learn that much of the history in that film is accurate. Méliès was first a magician who plied his trade at the theater he bought from the widow of illusionist Jean-Eugène Robert-Houdin (from whom Harry Houdini took his name). For 20 years after his exposure to the films of the Lumière Brothers in 1895, Méliès wrote, directed, and starred in hundreds of films created by his Star Film company, where he incorporated illusions into his own filmmaking. One of the first films made by Méliès showed him onstage making a woman disappear in an early example of stop-action photography. He was also known for combining multiple takes into a single collage in a technique known as superimposition.

After the outbreak of World War I, interest in Méliès' films largely disappeared, and he was forced to shut down his film company. In 1923, he sold the theater and his glass-enclosed studio in Montreuil and destroyed or sold off his film negatives. He did later operate a toy stand, although *Hugo*puts it in Gare du Nord whereas it was actually in Gare Montparnasse.

The museum displays early film equipment, including the Cinématographe and Kinetoscope, as well as objects associated with Méliès, such as magic equipment, his personal 35mm film camera, film costumes, posters, and models. Enjoy the entire 1902 film *A Trip to the Moon*, Méliès' masterpiece – both a special effects marvel and, at 13 minutes, a very long movie for its time.

Address 51 rue de Bercy, 75012 Paris, +33 (0)1 71 19 33 33, www.cinematheque.fr | Getting there Metro to Bercy (Lines 6, 14); bus 24, 71, 215 to Bercy–Aréna | Hours Mon, Wed–Fri noon–7pm, Sat & Sun 11am–8pm | Tip Directly across the Parc de Bercy, the Passarelle Simone de Beauvoir is a very cool, wavy pedestrian footbridge that opened in 2006 and connects the park with the National Library of France on the other side of the Seine.

# 70 MEP

*Photography from 1950 to the present day*

Often described as the world capital of photography, Paris is a city of celebrities like Man Ray and Germaine Krull. As a testament to the dynamic relationship between the city and the art of photography, Henry Chapier and Jean-Luc Monterosso founded the Paris Audio-visual association in 1979, which became the Maison Européenne de la Photographie (MEP) in 1996.

The MEP is the primary institution in France dedicated to photography in all its forms. Its collection is curated around international photographs and artists' films from the 1950s to the present day, in line with a mission to position contemporary photography at the heart of all the arts. The MEP's collection boasts an impressive array of 24,000 images, reflecting the institution's DNA for diversity. It encompasses fashion photography, photojournalism, documentary photography, and visual art.

The MEP organizes two temporary exhibitions at a time: one retrospective or thematic and one of an emerging artist. It is committed to showcasing original and relevant works by artists from different continents and backgrounds around themes that deal with issues touching on the preoccupations of our time. One such exhibition was "Love Song," which delved into the exploration of intimacy. Exhibitions are an opportunity to display MEP photographs in innovative ways, inviting contemporary artists to participate and fostering collaborations. The retrospective exhibitions feature artists of international renown who, despite their acclaim, have yet to receive a retrospective in Paris.

One of the key missions of the MEP is the allocation of space to little-known or unknown photographers, and there is an exhibit from an emerging artist every six weeks. Beyond exhibitions, the MEP functions as a research center, housing a library boasting over 30,000 books and offering a rich cultural program to engage and inspire you.

Address 5/7 rue de Fourcy, 75004 Paris, +33 (0)1 44 78 75 00, www.mep-fr.org | Getting there Metro to Saint-Paul (Line 1), Pont Marie (Line 7), Hotel de Ville (Line 11); bus 69, 76, 96 to Saint-Paul | Hours Wed & Fri 11am – 8pm, Thu 11am – 10pm, Sat & Sun 10am – 8pm | Tip Le Village Saint-Paul is a pedestrian haven and temple for shoppers who love unusual objects. Wander among the tiny antique and designer shops in the newly renovated interior space (Rue Saint Paul, www.levillagesaintpaul.com).

# 71 Mineralogy Museum

*Our planet's hidden treasures*

Whether or not you're a mineralogy expert, the Mineralogy Museum is sure to captivate you with the beauty of the treasures created by our planet. The Museum, nestled in the prestigious École des Mines on the edge of the Jardin du Luxembourg, is a treasure chest with one of the most comprehensive collections of minerals, holding over 100,000 cataloged samples from all around the world, including more than 4,000 pieces on display.

As you enter the museum, you will ascend the magnificent staircase of the Hôtel Vendôme. From there, you'll walk through a series of rooms, each adorned with period display cases filled with often brightly colored specimens. This spot marks the beginning of your visit, whether you choose to follow a designated itinerary or join a guided tour led by an expert (advance booking required).

As you continue your visit through the museum, you will realize the profound significance of certain mineral discoveries and the pivotal role they played in shaping human civilization. Take copper, for example. What purpose does it serve beyond conducting electricity? By heating it, we can make bowls and axes. But native copper is rare, which introduced the idea of scarcity, and that's where the story of humanity begins. How did human beings resolve this problem? A docent or guide will enlighten you with captivating stories of discoveries that have transformed our world in the past and continue to shape it today.

You will gain a deeper understanding of the impact of minerals on our daily lives, the political, social, and economic implications associated with them, as well as the environmental consequences. The mission of the museum is to provide a comprehensive array of arguments and insights to stimulate thought and conversations on these matters. And above all, don't leave the museum without first touching the Moon and Mars!

Address 60 boulevard Saint Michel, 75006 Paris, www.musee.mines-paristech.fr, musee@mines-paristech.fr | Getting there Metro to Odéon (Line 4), Cluny-La Sorbonne (Line 10), Raspail (Line 6); RER B to Luxembourg; bus 21, 27, 38, 82, 84, 85, 89 to Luxembourg | Hours Tue 10am–noon & 1:30–6pm, Wed–Fri 1:30–6pm, Sat 10am–12:30pm & 2–5pm | Tip If you are passionate about minerals, go see the collection at the Sorbonne University, one of the oldest in France (4 place Jussieu, www.collection-mineraux.sorbonne-universite.fr/fr/index.html).

# 72 Montmartre Museum

*The village during the Belle Époque*

Montmartre is a landmark neighborhood in the history of art. Many artists have called it home, including Auguste Renoir, Raoul Dufy, Suzanne Valadon, and Maurice Utrillo. The Montmartre Museum was founded in 1960 and is located in the 17th-century Maison du Bel Air, one of the oldest buildings in Montmartre. The museum houses a collection of paintings, posters, and drawings that depict the history of Montmartre in the 19th and 20th centuries. The experience is an immersion into the effervescence of the local studios from Bateau-Lavoir to Cortot and the ambience of its famous cabarets like Le Chat Noir and the Moulin Rouge.

Montmartre was a meeting place for the artistic community. Artists loved it here because it was a goldmine for subjects we would now call modern and a limitless source of inspiration. You get a real sense of the bohemian atmosphere at the Maison Bel Air when you visit Suzanne Valadon's studio/apartment and the bedroom of her son Maurice Utrillo, which are preserved in their original state. The room covering the Chat Noir cabaret transports us to the 19th-century party scene. Founded by Rodolphe Salis, the Chat Noir was an extravagant and whimsical place, where you could play the piano or recite poetry. Henri de Toulouse-Lautrec, Erik Satie, Alphonse Allais, Camille Pissarro, and Vincent Van Gogh were regulars.

Henri Rivière opened his "shadow theater" at the Chat Noir. This was a predecessor to cinema and a real innovation for the time. Zinc silhouettes illuminated behind a white canvas screen entertained an audience of artists and intellectuals. Rodolphe Salis commented on the plot, musicians offered accompaniment, and everything, from the story to the music, was improvised.

The Montmartre Museum brings the Belle Époque back to life. This was a time when the arts and parties were celebrated and when the thirst for freedom and change was palpable.

Address 12 rue Cortot, 75018 Paris, +33 (0)1 49 25 89 39, www.museedemontmartre.fr, infos@museedemontmartre.fr | Getting there Metro to Lamarck-Caulaincourt (Line 12), Anvers (Line 2); bus 40 to Saules-Cortot | Hours Daily 10am–7pm | Tip Take a detour to the cobblestoned street Impasse de la Villa Léandre. Look for the Hôtel Lejeune and the private mansion of Romanian poet Tristan Tzara (no. 15), both listed as historical monuments (just off avenue Junot at rue Simon Dereure).

# 73_Mundolingua

*A riddle wrapped in a mystery inside an enigma*

It appears remarkably small for a machine that was so integral to the course of World War II, and since most were destroyed at the end of the war, it is very rare to find an example today. Behind a curtain of chicken wire in a corner of Mundolingua, the museum of language, sits an authentic German Enigma machine.

Just a bit larger than a manual typewriter, Enigma was developed in Germany in the 1920s and used to encrypt commercial, diplomatic, and military communications throughout the war. Polish and later English mathematicians were able to decrypt the messages sent through Enigma machines, and their efforts are credited with shortening the war. But the amazing story behind Enigma remains, and coding and encryption are just one of the many aspects of language explored at the museum.

Mundolingua approaches language thematically, and each theme is explored in multiple languages through rich, multimedia displays comprising signage, interactive computer exercises, and artifacts like the Rosetta Stone or an early Edison phonograph. Explore the family tree of languages and learn about endangered and extinct branches. Discover the linguistic and cultural origins of writing systems, Braille, sign languages, and curse words. Practice invented languages like Klingon. Listen to similar vowel sounds in many languages and see where they originate in different parts of the head and throat. Examine all the bits of technology that make up a two-story Tower of Babel.

Will you linger in the library or the four-seat video theater? Or perhaps you would rather play a word-based board game or a room-sized version of Scrabble with your family and friends. What appears at first to be a short, pleasant visit to a museum of language quickly turns into a fascinating journey where you will spend hours exploring the many different facets of culture and communication.

Address 10 rue Servandoni, 75006 Paris, +33 (0)1 56 81 65 79, www.mundolingua.org, contact@mundolingua.org | Getting there Metro to Saint-Sulpice (Line 4), Mabillon (Line 10), Sèvres-Babylone (Line 12); bus 58, 84, 89 to Senat or Musée du Luxembourg | Hours Sat–Wed 10am–7pm; Thu & Fri by appointment | Tip Study French or attend one of the many cultural events at the Alliance Française (101 boulevard Raspail, www.alliancefr.org).

# 74 The Museum of Chocolate

*Feeding and educating chocoholics*

Somewhere near the introduction of molds into the industry, you will realize that you have eaten way too much chocolate. Dispensers filled with milk, dark, and white chocolate disks are placed strategically throughout Choco-Story Paris, the Museum of Chocolate, and they are one of the perks of your visit to this shrine to deliciousness.

An initiative of the Van Belle family of Belgium, this museum explores the origins and evolution of chocolate on three floors on the Boulevard de Bonne Nouvelle. The first floor explains the science of the cacao tree and the importance of cacao in the history of both Mayan and Aztec cultures, who turned it into a savory drink with roasted corn and water. As a source of currency as well as a drink, cacao was considered a "divine nectar." The museum houses an impressive collection of sculpture and utensils, including several *metate*used to grind cacao beans into powder.

In the early 16th century, Spain conquered the Aztecs and brought cocoa back to Europe, where it was later combined with sugar to create the sweet sensation we know today. Once you make your way to the second floor, you are introduced to this transformation, beginning with the addition of sugar as shavings from solid chunks of molded cane sugar.

You'll continue to follow the evolution of chocolate from a drink of the European royal courts to mass consumption in the 19th and 20th centuries. Along the way, there are collections of special porcelain and silver drinkware, early chocolate molds, mass production equipment, and finally, 20th century labels and advertising materials. For young visitors, the museum summarizes each story through a series of dioramas placed thoughtfully in the walls at a child's height.

Your visit ends with a truffle-making demo and the largest chocolate Eiffel Tower you'll ever see – and an upset stomach, if you're not careful.

Address 28 boulevard de Bonne Nouvelle, 75010 Paris, +33 (0)1 42 29 68 60, www.museeduchocolat.fr, info@museeduchocolat.fr | Getting there Metro to Bonne Nouvelle (Lines 8, 9); bus 20, 32, 39 to Poissonnière-Bonne Nouvelle | Hours Daily 10am–6pm | Tip You can smell the wonderful aroma of fine chocolate emanating into the street at the factory store of Alain Ducasse (40 rue de la Roquette, www.lechocolat-alainducasse.com).

# 75 Museum of Decorative Arts

*Conservatory of the genius of artisans and artists*

Located in the Louvre Palace, the Museum of Decorative Arts was created over 150 years ago by collectors, industrialists, and artisans who shared a common concern for the quality of everyday objects. The collection, one of the largest in the world, presents a vast array of applied artistic production from the Middle Ages to the present day, encompassing furniture, glass, ceramics, and even advertising. Known for its Period Rooms, which provide immersive experiences into various historical settings, the museum has recently refurbished and enhanced its Art Nouveau collection to showcase the artistic and interior design revolution that took place in France around 1900.

The collection here differs from what can be seen in other museums because it features works by French Art Nouveau artists who are not represented elsewhere. It brings together furniture sets, ceramics, glassware, goldsmithing, paintings, stained-glass windows, wallpapers, and posters. Interior design was paramount to proponents of Art Nouveau, who saw it as a space where modern men and women could thrive and achieve fulfillment.

The Art Nouveau style drew inspiration from two sources. First was the influence of Japan, which reopened its borders in 1850, and created a revolution among French artists introducing new creative approaches and a fresh perspective on nature. Second was the influence of a French classical tradition, particularly the Louis XV style, with its luscious floral motifs. When cabinetmaker and decorator Louis Majorelle began crafting furniture, he drew inspiration from this classical tradition, resulting in marquetry masterpieces.

The museum shows that within merely 5 years (1900–1905), an impressive diversity of artistic production emerged in the French Art Nouveau movement, defying existing perceptions with its richness.

Address 107 rue de Rivoli, 75001 Paris, +33 (0)1 44 55 57 50, www.madparis.fr | Getting there Metro to Palais Royal (Lines 1, 7); bus 21, 69, 72 to Palais Royal-Musée du Louvre | Hours Tue – Sun 11am – 6pm | Tip Step inside another era on a stroll through the wonderful Galerie Vivienne, built in 1823 and listed as a historic monument (4 rue des Petits Champs).

# 76 Museum of Jewish Art and History

*The long, rich history of Jews in France*

Evidenced by the numerous memorials across Paris, the history of the Jewish community is inextricably tied to the Holocaust. The Museum of Jewish Art and History does indeed have an exhibit on Jewish life in Paris in 1939. However, the historic Hôtel de Saint-Aignan, which had once housed the shops of Jewish immigrant merchants and craftsmen, now provides an even richer understanding of Judaism.

The Introductory Room attests to the permanence of Hebrew and the importance of the written word, highlighting fundamental religious and cultural traditions and the community's geographical dispersion. As if to underscore the longtime presence of Jews in Paris, there is a prominent display of 13th century funerary stelae that came from one of the Jewish cemeteries that existed on the Left Bank in the Middle Ages. Other museum artifacts date as far back as the 3rd century.

The museum is organized both chronologically and thematically. Each era or theme has a panel with a detailed explanation of a historical period or religious or cultural tradition and its origins and importance. For the non-Jewish visitor in particular, these explanations provide context for the accompanying paintings, manuscripts, and objects. If you are unfamiliar with Sukkot, for example, the theme of pilgrimage teaches you that the Feast of Tabernacles commemorates the 40 years spent in the wilderness after the exodus from Egypt. Traditionally, Jews are supposed to eat, entertain, and even sleep for seven days in a *sukkah*, or temporary hut, with a roof of branches to see the sky. The first object acquired by the museum was an exquisite 19th-century *sukkah*constructed from 36 numbered wooden panels. Its interior is brilliantly painted with a landscape of Jerusalem, the countryside around Lake Constance, part of the Ten Commandments, and a floral motif that alludes to the harvest.

Address Hôtel de Saint-Aignan, 71 rue Temple, 75003 Paris, +33 (0)1 53 01 86 60, www.mahj.org/fr | Getting there Metro to Rambuteau (Line 11), Hôtel de Ville (Line 1); RER A, B, D to Châtelet-Les Halles; bus 29, 38 to Centre Georges Pompidou, 75 to Archives-Rambuteau | Hours Tue, Thu, Fri 11am–6pm, Wed 11am–9pm, Sat & Sun 10am–7pm | Tip Walk by the Agoudas Hakehilos synagogue in the Marais, designed by Hector Guimard in 1913 in his famous art nouveau style (10 rue Pavée, pavee.fr).

# 77__Museum of Man

*An exploration of our humanity*

The Museum of Man began as an ethnographical museum in the 19th century, and for some Parisians, their familiarity with the museum's history is tied to its famous World War II Resistance group. A recent reimagining of the museum, still housed in the Chaillot Palace overlooking the Trocadero Gardens, has created one of the most compelling and photogenic institutions in Paris.

The museum's pedagogical mission seeks to answer three basic questions. Who are we? Where did we come from? Where are we headed? To answer these questions, the museum applies a multidisciplinary approach. Exhibits consider what sets us apart as humans: the effect of nature and culture on our physical bodies, our ability to think and understand our place in society, our faculty for reason, how we confront our mortality, and how we communicate with others through speech. You'll come to acknowledge our diversity of appearance while focusing on our common humanity.

One of the most effective and amusing exhibits is the striking red Wall of Languages covered in long, red tongues accompanying descriptions of individual languages. Pull a tongue to hear a snippet of that language. It's hard to resist pulling a lot of tongues and listening to many languages.

The second part of the museum explores our evolution highlighted by an impressive display of the bones of the successive proto-human species that resulted in today's homo sapiens, as well as later paleolithic and neolithic artifacts. On the top floor, the museum explores the effects of globalization and technology. In one display, industrial objects combine with natural materials to create a variety of traditional Senegalese protective amulets. Alongside amulets made from horns and hooves are those made from water bottles. The bed of a pair of flip-flops, in particular, is transformed with natural imagery and Islamic writings.

**Address** 17 place du Trocadéro, 75016 Paris, +33 (0)1 44 05 72 72, www.museedelhomme.fr | **Getting there** Metro to Trocadero (Lines 6, 9); bus 20, 22, 32, 63 to Trocadero | **Hours** Wed–Mon 11am–7pm | **Tip** The Paris Aquarium is just steps away in the Trocadero Gardens and features Europe's largest jellyfish zoo (5 avenue Albert de Mun, www.aquariumdeparis.com).

# 78 Museum of Modern Art

*A different approach to modern and contemporary art*

The Museum of Modern Art is an unusual museum built in the form of a palace for the 1937 World Expo. Recently renovated, it has been returned to its original architecture. This museum presents modern and contemporary art collections and focuses on major artistic movements from the 20th century to the current scene, illustrated by major figures in art history, as well as lesser-known artists. By deviating from conventional notions of art history and showcasing what is not seen elsewhere, the museum aims to surprise visitors with little-known and occasionally unsettling works, while also reminding us of the role of Paris in recent art history.

Many of the works on display have an intimate connection to the museum's own history. It has rare, site-specific works such as *La Danse inachevée* (1931), an unfinished piece by Henri Matisse. In 1930, Matisse accepted a commission to create a mural for the Barnes Foundation, his first project to integrate a monumental work within an architectural context. He chose the theme of dance but was dissatisfied with his first attempt, leading him to work on a second rendition known as *La Danse*.

However, this work was too large, prompting him to produce a third variation. In 1990, Matisse's heirs made an extraordinary discovery when they uncovered the preparatory elements destined for the three monumental pieces of *La Danse inachevée*. Today, both *La Danse inachevée* and *La Danse* are on display at the museum. *La Danse* consists of eleven plates with black, pink, and blue cut-out gouache paintings. It depicts the fragmented bodies of nymphs that draw viewers into the rhythm of their dance.

Another fascinating site-specific work is Niele Toroni's *Cabinet de peinture*, a conceptual piece that plays with the space and light of an off-kilter room, effectively immersing you as if you were stepping into the artwork itself.

Address 11 Avenue du Président Wilson, 75116 Paris, +33 (0)1 53 67 40 00, www.mam.paris.fr | Getting there Metro to Alma-Marceau/Iéna (Line 9); bus 32, 82 to Iéna, 72 to Musée d'Art Moderne, 42, 80, 92 to Alma-Marceau | Hours Tue–Sun 10am–6pm | Tip Take a break at Carette tea and pastry shop, a Place du Trocadero institution since 1927 known for its macarons (4 place du Trocadero, www.facebook.com/CarettePatisserie).

# 79 Museum of Music

*The double bass on steroids*

For lovers of music and musical instruments, the Museum of Music is a fascinating exploration of 400 years of mostly Western music. Starting with the instruments used in Monteverdi's opera *Orpheus*, the museum showcases over 1,000 objects. Each floor highlights a new century until you reach the 20th century and its jazz instruments, electric guitars, and electronic music.

Along the way, there are hundreds of woodwind and brass instruments, including period pieces that resemble serpents and piping more complicated than today's versions of the same instruments. Listen to music samples wherever possible, so you'll know what a transverse flute or a 17th-century harpsichord sound like.

Did you know that there are three main types of string instruments? Some are plucked, like harps, lutes, and guitars. Some have bows drawn over them, like violins and cellos. And some require hammers to strike the strings, like harpsichords and pianos. The museum's row of beautiful harps, as well as stunning, early Italian pianos, serve as an introduction to the musical adventure. Were you aware that Stradivarius made more than just violins? Alongside his violins and those from other famous luthiers like Guarneri and Lupot, the museum displays something exceedingly rare: a Stradivarius guitar.

The 19th century was a period of great innovation. Pleyel and Erard pianos made France the epicenter of piano making. Orchestras added more instruments to create fuller sounds for new concert halls. And new instruments like the saxophone and accordion were invented. Perhaps the most outrageous instrument was the 11.5-foot-tall (3.5-meter) Octobass of Jean-Baptiste Vuillaume. While resembling a huge double bass, the octobass required a step so that the musician could reach the keys used to create different notes. The museum has one of only two surviving examples of this dramatic and powerful instrument.

**Address** Cité de la Musique-Philharmonie de Paris, 221 avenue Jean-Jaurès, 75019 Paris, +33 (0)1 44 84 44 84, philharmoniedeparis.fr/fr/musee-de-la-musique, musee@philharmoniedeparis.fr | **Getting there** Metro to Porte de Pantin (Line 5); tramway to Porte de Pantin (Line 3b); bus 75, 151 to Porte de Pantin | **Hours** Tue–Fri noon–6pm, Sat & Sun 10am–6pm | **Tip** La Salle Pleyel was the home of the Philharmonie de Paris until 2015. Today, it offers more contemporary music events (252 rue du Faubourg Saint-Honoré, www.sallepleyel.com).

# 80 Museum of Relief Maps

*A visual warning to France's enemies*

Don't even think about invading France.

That's the message any foreign diplomat would have heard loud and clear strolling through the collection of relief maps at the Louvre in the late 17th century. Created by Louis XIV to plan against both invaders and domestic uprisings, these relief maps displayed the defenses of fortified towns and chateaus through the country.

The French State continued to create these relief maps until the late 19th century, when they were replaced by other map-making techniques. Today, a collection of several dozen maps can be seen at the Museum of Relief Maps on the top floor attic of Les Invalides.

Each relief map displays a different locale in striking detail. A series of small wooden tables, each with an individual segment of the map, are connected like giant puzzles to create a larger tableau. Some, like Bayonne, are dozens of square meters in size. Each 1/600 scale map shows the topography of a town and its surrounding farmland and waterways. Artisans faithfully copied street layouts and created individual buildings and trees. Most importantly, they documented the elaborate defenses laid out to protect a strategic location. Star-shaped forts provide ample space for artillery and are placed next to population centers to guard both sea and land approaches.

The most striking relief map at the museum may be the model of Mont Saint-Michel. Created by one of the monks who lived in the abbey, this relief map recreates the island's steep layout and its many buildings in minute detail. The model of the church opens to show its interior and, if you look carefully, you can see tiny figures in the windows of some buildings. This model, along with its companions, was hidden in a storage facility during World War II. More recent restorations have revealed that at some point it served as a cozy home for a family of rodents.

Address Hôtel National des Invalides, 129 rue de Grenelle, 75007 Paris, +33 (0)1 45 51 92 45, www.museedesplansreliefs.culture.fr | Getting there Metro to La Tour-Marbourg (Line 8), Saint François-Xavier (Line 13), Varenne (Line 13); RER C to Invalides; bus 28 to Invalide-La Tour Marbourg, 69 to Esplanade des Invalides, 89, 92 to Vauban-Hôtel des Invalides | Hours Apr 1–Sep 30 daily 10am–6pm, Oct 1–Mar 31 daily 10am–5pm | Tip A wonderful tribute to French charcuterie in all its forms can be experienced nearby at restaurant Arnaud Nicolas (4 avenue de la Bourdonnais, www.arnaudnicolas.paris).

# 81 Museum of Romantic Life

*Discovering 19th-century romanticism*

As you wander down the discrete alley that leads to the house of artist Ary Scheffer (1795–1858), you get the impression that the owner has invited you for a visit. Ary Scheffer, a renowned Dutch painter, was a notable host to prominent figures of the Romantic movement, including George Sand, Frédéric Chopin, Eugène Delacroix, Alfred de Vigny, and many others.

The artist and his family moved to Paris' New Athens district in 1811. This neighborhood was a thriving hub for artists, writers, and musicians, and Scheffer soon found himself immersed in French political and artistic life. He was introduced to the Duke of Orléans, the future King Louis Philippe, and taught drawing to his children. Scheffer embodied French Romanticism, and he was known for hosting Romantic artists, writers, and musicians in his studio on Friday evenings. This home was a hub for intellectual life in Romantic-era Paris. Guests would meet to listen to music or recite verses. Chopin, who preferred intimate performances over grand settings, liked to play here. Friendship and creativity went hand in hand.

Upon entering the studio-lounge, you will feel as though you are immersed in an evening with the Romantics. Scheffer's piano, library, stove, and paintings are a testimony to this bygone era. His home, which still features period decorations, lets visitors admire works by the owner and his contemporaries. Crushed watercolor landscapes created by George Sand are on display, as well as the *Album Liber Amicorum de Rachel,* which contains the heartfelt words from friends of the actress Rachel. Every corner of the museum reflects the Romantic movement's deep commitment to fostering artistic fraternity.

Don't miss a visit to Rose Bakery, the tearoom nestled within the museum's garden and greenhouse. It offers a slice of paradise along with some of the most delectable cakes in Paris.

Address Hotel Scheffer-Renan, 16 rue Chaptal, 75009 Paris, +33 (0)1 55 31 95 67, www.museevieromantique.paris.fr | Getting there Metro to Saint-Georges (Line 12), Pigalle (Line 2) | Hours Tue – Sun 10am – 6pm | Tip Seek out the plaque marking George Sand's birthplace in the 3rd Arrondissement (46 Rue Meslay).

# 82 Museum of the 1930s

*Art and culture between the World Wars*

The Museum of the 1930s actually covers the entire period between the World Wars. Boulogne and Billancourt had combined into one Parisian suburb by the 1920s.

Automotive and aviation pioneers had established major presences here, followed by artists and architects, who set up their ateliers and residences here as well. The museum presents several artistic currents of the interwar period, including art deco, cubism, the School of Paris, and modernism.

You will find a large collection from furniture designer and assembler Jacques-Émile Ruhlmann that includes not only his distinctive furniture, but also some of his drawings and his personal reference books. Ruhlmann was an integral part of the 1925 Exhibition of Modern Decorative and Industrial Arts that birthed the art deco movement. He designed high-end furniture made of ebony, ivory, and velvet that were sold at luxury stores such as Printemps.

The sculptor Joseph Bernard, who exhibited at Ruhlmann's gallery in 1924, had settled in Boulogne in a workshop built by Charles Plumet, the chief architect of the 1925 Exhibition. In 1926, Ruhlmann produced a furniture set for Bernard's home on avenue Robert-Schuman. For this set, Ruhlmann eschewed luxurious materials and instead used simple, raw wood without inlay or marquetry. The furniture's only decorations are the bronze locks designed by the sculptor himself.

In addition to Ruhlmann, Bernard, and works by other artists such as Lipchitz, Orloff, and Denis, the museum has an important collection from artists who traveled to the French colonies on awards and scholarships, as well as indigenous artists. Painter Alexander Iackovleff also accompanied colonial expeditions across Africa and Asia launched by Citroën in the 1920s and 1930s. The museum also exhibits the works of artists from the colonies in order to bring this little-known part of art history to light.

Address 26 avenue André Morizet, 92100 Boulogne-Billancourt, +33 (0)1 55 18 53 00, www.boulognebillancourt.com/loisirs/culture/musees/musee-des-annees-30 | Getting there Metro to Marcel Sembat (Line 9); bus 126, 175 to Hôtel de Ville | Hours Tue–Sun 11am–6pm | Tip A small museum dedicated to the Polish French sculptor Paul Landowski, best known for the monumental statue of *Christ the Redeemer*in Rio de Janeiro, is located in the same building.

# 83 Museum of the Liberation of Paris

*The heroic struggle for freedom from tyranny*

On August 25, 2019, Paris celebrated the 75th anniversary of the Liberation of Paris with a new museum dedicated to the event, General Jacques-Philippe Leclerc, and resistance hero Jean Moulin. The museum's location, its treatment of the Nazi occupation and the French resistance, and its free admission make this one of the most compelling museums in the city.

The museum is housed in one of two 18th-century toll houses located directly above the former bunker command station of Colonel Henri Roy-Tanguy, head of the Parisian Resistance forces. If you can walk down and up the 100 steps, the mixed reality experience introduces you to the colonel and other resistance fighters and teaches you how to make a street barricade.

The museum itself covers the occupation from 1940 through to the week of the Liberation in August 1944. You'll learn about Moulin and others who fought a clandestine war against the occupation, as well as Leclerc and the Free French 2nd Army. Nazi propaganda posters, stories of resistance fights and soldiers, and moving video interviews fill the route leading up to a room dedicated to the Liberation of Paris. Each day's events during the week of August 19 are recounted in detail, starting with the leaflet calling on all Parisians to fight, and continuing to the stories of street battles, the Nazi surrender to Leclerc's troops, and General de Gaulle's arrival in Paris.

During the Occupation, Parisian Marguerite Sabaut made a dress decorated with several Parisian monuments, hoping to wear it one day with its matching earrings and a purse with the Cross of Lorraine, the symbol of Free France. Madame Sabaut got to wear her ensemble to the parade on the Champs-Elysées on August 26. These are some of the many poignant mementos of the Liberation.

**Address** 4 Avenue du Colonel Henri Rol-Tanguy, 75014 Paris, +33 (0)1 40 64 39 44, www.museeliberation-leclerc-moulin.paris.fr, museeML@paris.fr | **Getting there** Metro to Denfert-Rochereau (Lines 4, 6); RER B to Denfert-Rochereau; bus 38, 59, 68, 88 to Denfert-Rochereau | **Hours** Tue–Sun 10am–6pm | **Tip** A plaque on the wall of the Hôtel Dieu hospital commemorates the death on August 19, 1944 of Rey Marcel, brigadier of the National Police. It is one of many plaques throughout Paris honoring those who died during the Liberation (corner of Parvis Notre Dame and Rue d'Arcole).

# 84 Museum of the Order of the Liberation

*Stories of individual and collective heroism*

The Museum of the Order of the Liberation is a testament to the bravery and patriotism of the French people during one of the most difficult times. The Order was started in late 1940 by General de Gaulle to honor those who displayed valor fighting against the Axis powers abroad and resisting the Nazi occupiers and the Vichy regime in France.

The Order's members, the Compagnons, received the Cross of the Liberation. They were men and women from all sectors of society, as well as several fighting units and five French cities. Using words, photos, and video testimony, uniforms, flags, and personal artifacts, the museum shares the stories of over 1,000 heroes to explain how France continued to wage war following the June 1940 armistice. All their stories are powerful and moving.

Jacques Joubert des Ouches started training as a pilot while he was a student. He left France aboard a lobster boat to England just before the armistice. He fought with the Free French Air Forces and then completed his training in England, flying with several British squadrons before joining the 2/2 Berry hunting group in early 1944. After 160 missions, he disappeared off the Normandy coast on D-Day. Today, there is a marker where he is believed to have crashed at Utah Beach. You'll see his badges and his personal mascot, a doll of a sailor from the SS *Empress of Australia*, a troop transport ship.

Henri Fertet was one of the youngest Compagnons when he joined the Resistance in 1942 at the age of 15. Over the next year, he led three operations against the Nazis. He was arrested in July 1943 and executed by firing squad later in September. On the day of his execution, he drafted a touching letter to his parents in which he wrote, "I die for my country. I want a free France and happy French people." He ended with, "Death calls me.... A thousand kisses. Vive la France."

Address Hôtel National des Invalides, 129 rue de Grenelle, 75007 Paris, +33 (0)1 47 05 35 15, www.ordredelaliberation.fr | Getting there Metro to La Tour-Marbourg (Line 8), Saint François-Xavier (Line 13), Varenne (Line 13); RER C to Invalides; bus 28 to Invalide-La Tour Marbourg, 69 to Esplanade des Invalides, 89, 92 to Vauban-Hôtel des Invalides | Hours Daily 10am–6pm | Tip On quai Henri IV between the entrance to the Port d'Arsenal and rue de Schomberg is the Esplanade des Villes Compagnons de la Libération, where there are plaques that pay hommage to six women Compagnons.

# 85_National Archives Museum

*France's memory bank*

The National Archives Museum is located in the Hôtel de Soubise and Hôtel de Rohan. More than a museum, the space is a historic home that was built and inhabited by the noble Guise and Rohan-Soubise families from the 14th to the 18th centuries. The stately entrance is the largest of its kind in Paris, and today, public records are preserved here. This museum is a memory bank of French history, featuring priceless archives and opulent interiors.

Created during the French Revolution, the National Archives preserves materials from France's various political regimes from the 7th century to the present day. In 1808, Napoleon Bonaparte selected the Hôtel de Soubise for the documents, books, and artifacts and initiated a construction program to accommodate the expanding collection. The Hôtel de Soubise only preserves papers from before the French Revolution, and the large rooms now host the National Archives Museum. Stroll through the building's vast reception spaces to view major documents chronicling the history of France, including the Edict of Nantes signed by Henri IV in 1598, and Marie Antoinette's final letter.

Exhibits rotate every four months to preserve these historical treasures. Admire sumptuously furnished spaces decorated in the Rococo style by Germain Boffrand, as well as the bedroom of the Princess of Soubise and a reconstruction of an archivist's studio, including files, storage boxes, and shelves, and one of the archive rooms. The crown jewel of the museum is the "Iron Cabinet," which contains all of France's constitutions, alongside documents of high historical value, including the Declaration of the Rights of Man and of the Citizen. This space is only open to the public on special occasions, notably the Heritage Days, or the Journées du Patrimoine. A visit to this museum promises an exceptional experience for history enthusiasts.

**Address** 60 rue des Francs Bourgeois, 75003 Paris, +33 (0)1 40 27 60 96, www.archives-nationales.culture.gouv.fr/fr/web/guest/musee, infomusee.archivesnationales@culture.gouv.fr | **Getting there** Metro to Hôtel de Ville (Line 1), Rambuteau (Line 11), Arts et Metiers (Line 3); bus 29, 75 to Archives-Haudriettes or Archives-Rambuteau | **Hours** Mon, Wed–Fri 10am–5:30pm, Sat & Sun 2–5:30pm | **Tip** Take a stroll through the National Archives' extraordinary grounds. There's something here for everyone, from the classic 18th-century French garden to the well-tended orchard and the romantic 19th-century park.

# 86 Nissim de Camondo Museum

*An intimate peek into a collector's home*

The Nissim de Camondo Museum is situated in a superb mansion that was built on the edge of Parc Monceau in 1911 by the architect René Sergent for Count Moïse de Camondo (1860–1935). Born into a powerful banking family, the count had the mansion built to house his exceptional collection of French decorative art from the second half of the 18th century. He would donate the home and the collection to the French State in 1935 in memory of his son and heir apparent Nissim de Camondo (1892–1917), who died in combat during World War I. Perfectly preserved, the home is equipped with the latest modern comforts of the early 20th century.

The collection includes prestigious furniture by renowned cabinet makers, including Jean-Francois Œben, Jean Henri Riesner, Jean-Baptiste-Claude Sené, Adam Weisweiler, and Georges Jacob. It also features paintings by notable artists, such as Hubert Robert, Robert Demachy, and Francesco Guardi, as well as painted panels by Jean-Baptiste Huet, Sèvres porcelain, and Gobelin tapestries. Until his passing in 1935, Count Moïse de Camondo continued to acquire artworks with a commitment to perfection and harmony.

Hidden beneath the opulent décor, the latest in modern comforts – indirect lighting, elevators, and a telephone – were skillfully and discreetly installed. All the rooms in the house have been impeccably preserved, from the ceremonial lounges and private apartments with their modern bathrooms, to the staff room and, notably, the kitchen.

The kitchen is located in the semi-basement, which was the prevailing custom in large, 19th-century residences. It boasts a modern style with white tiled floors and cast iron coal stoves. It has been meticulously designed to optimize organization and minimize the cook's movements. One cannot help but dream of having a kitchen as splendid as this!

Address 63 rue de Monceau, 75008 Paris, +33 (0)1 44 55 57 50, www.madparis.fr/Musee-Nissim-de-Camondo-125 | Getting there Metro to Monceau (Line 2), Villiers (Lines 2, 3); bus 20, 30, 93 to Malesherbes/Courcelles, 84 to Ruysdaël | Hours Wed – Sun 10am – 5:30pm | Tip Visit nearby art galleries in that present stunning contemporary artworks to the public, including the Hopkins (2 avenue Matignon), Lelong (38 avenue Matignon), Gagosian (4 rue de Ponthieu), and Emmanuel Perrotin (2 bis avenue Matignon).

# 87_The Orangerie Museum

*Rare works of art*

The Orangerie Museum did not always display works of art. It was originally built in 1852 to shelter the orange trees that adorned the garden of the Palais des Tuileries during the winter months. The south side of the building is made of glass to let in the sunlight, while the north side is walled off to block the wind. As a result, the space features incredible natural light. In 1921, management of the building was transferred to the Beaux-Arts Administration of Paris. Today, it is home to Claude Monet's Water Lilies (1840–1926) and the Jean Walter and Paul Guillaume collection. The rarity of the works displayed here makes it one of the most important museums of painted works in Paris.

It became an exhibition space in 1921. Georges Clemenceau (1841–1929) proposed the installation of Claude Monet's *Water Lilies* mural, which Monet had generously given to the French government as a symbol of peace following the armistice of 1918. This ensemble work is one of the largest monumental paintings of the first half of the 20th century. In the natural light, you'll discover Monet's *Water Lilies* cycle, eight canvases that immerse you in his ethereal and expansive Giverny garden in Normandy, where Monet spent thirty years exploring all the variations of light. He participated in the layout design of the museum's two oval rooms that would house his massive works. The curve of the walls invites contemplation.

The Jean Walter and Paul Guillaume collection is one of the most beautiful bodies of works in Europe, consisting of 146 pieces from 1860 to the 1930s. It was mainly curated by the art dealer Paul Guillaume and acquired by the French State in the late 1950s. You will see works by such luminaries as Renoir, Cézanne, Gauguin, Sisley, Modigliani, Matisse, and Picasso, among other masters. Temporary exhibitions are organized throughout the year with themes covering Impressionists to contemporary art.

**Address** Jardin des Tuileries, Place de la Concorde, 75001 Paris, +33 (0)1 44 77 80 07, www.musee-orangerie.fr | **Getting there** Metro to Concorde (Lines 1, 8, 12); bus 42, 45, 52, 72, 73, 84, 94 to Concorde | **Hours** Wed–Mon 9am–6pm | **Tip** Claude Monet lived for some years in a studio at Place Furstenberg, a small corner of paradise of Saint-Germain-des-Prés and what is today the favored location for interior decorators.

# 88_The Orsay Museum

*Impressionists and much more*

The Musée d'Orsay is home to an art collection ranging from 1848 to 1914, a period when realism, Impressionism, Art Nouveau, and other important movements emerged. Renowned for its exceptional collection of Impressionist works, the museum also offers a trail of sculptures installed beneath the glass roof of the former Belle Époque train station. Among the notable sculptures on display are *La Liberté* by Auguste Bartholdi, a scale version of Lady Liberty in New York Harbor, and *La Danse* (1869) by Jean-Baptiste Carpeaux (1827–1875). Carpeaux was one of the most significant sculptors of the second half of the 19th century. His genius is expressed through *La Danse*, one of the most scandalous works of the 19th century.

*La Danse* is part of a high relief commissioned for the façade of the Opéra Garnier. Charles Garnier, then a young architect, asked his former school friend to create one of four sculptures. Carpeaux conceived a composition featuring bacchantes, followers of Bacchus, swirling around a young male "genius." This masterpiece captivates viewers through the dynamic and restrained movement of the bacchantes, emanating from the body of the genius. However, the genius's exposed torso provoked an impassioned letter from an unknown admirer, who sought information on where she could meet the man who served as the artist's model. The groups of sculptures on the Opéra's façade were unveiled in late 1869.

Carpeaux's bold group immediately stood out amidst the more subdued nature of the other three sculptures. People called it obscene and an affront to public morality and said it reminded them of a brothel. One night, a bottle of black ink was thrown at one of the bacchantes. Garnier received hundreds of insulting letters. To save the statue, Carpeaux turned to Napoleon III to no avail. But when the Franco-Prussian war broke out in 1870, the ordeal was forgotten.

**Address** 1 rue de la Légion d'Honneur 75007 Paris, +33 (0)1 40 49 48 14, www.musee-orsay.fr | **Getting there** Metro to Solférino (Line 12); RER C to Musée d'Orsay; bus 68, 69, 73, 87 to Musée d'Orsay | **Hours** Tue & Wed, Fri–Sun 9:30am–6pm, Thu 9:30am–9:45pm | **Tip** Look for one of the most beautiful fountains in Paris, the Fontaine des Quatre Parties du Monde in the Jardin des Grands Explorateurs, opposite the Palais du Luxembourg, another example of Carpeaux' dynamic style and the whirling movement of the allegories (27M avenue de l'Observatoire, www.paris.fr).

# 89 Palais de Tokyo

*The anti-museum*

The Palais de Tokyo celebrated its 20th anniversary in 2022. Dedicated to the emerging art scene, the 22,300-square-meter (240,000-square-foot) center is not only the largest space for contemporary art in Europe, but also one of the continent's youngest cultural institutions, attracting a primarily youthful audience of 25 to 35 year-olds, especially with its late hours. The Palais de Tokyo stands out in the capital's museum landscape in many ways.

You'll find only temporary exhibitions here that reflect the diversity of creation from painting and sculpture installations to music, cinema, fashion, and design. Disciplines outside the scope of most museums find their home here, including comics, graphic design, video games, and science fiction. The Palais de Tokyo is an energetic and innovative space that organizes thematic and monographic exhibitions around emerging and established artists from France and abroad, including lectures, festivals, and other events that give ample freedom to its artists. This is an anti-museum par excellence. It is constantly changing and aims to challenge our perception of art and continually redefine it. But it does not stop there. Ecology is a key element in the museum's strategy, both in terms of the themes covered by exhibitions and their overall design.

The Palais de Tokyo was the first art center to establish a corporate social responsibility department, mobilizing financial sponsorship and expertise to create a positive carbon footprint. The museum designs its events around environmentally conscious principles, promotes biodiversity in its gardens, and seeks to rehabilitate its building in a more sustainable manner. It also places a strong emphasis on inclusion and education. As a true melting pot of artistic expression, the vibrant institution breaks down barriers between different artistic practices, fostering the emergence of new forms of expression within the heart of Paris.

Address 13 avenue du Président Wilson, 75016 Paris, +33 (0)1 81 97 35 88, www.palaisdetokyo.com | Getting there Metro to Iéna or Alma-Marceau (Line 9); RER C to Pont d'Alma; bus 63 to Iéna, 42, 80, 92 to Alma-Marceau, 72 to Musée d'Art Moderne-Palais de Tokyo | Hours Wed–Mon noon–9pm | Tip Art 42 is a street art and post-graffiti museum that showcases an extraordinary ensemble of 150 artworks. You'll find sculptures, stencils, collages, and more crafted by urban artists such as Banksy, JR, Shepard Fairey, Bault, Madame, and others (96 boulevard Bessières, www.art42.fr).

# 90 Paris Catacombs

*Messages to the living from the empire of the dead*

Once you descend the 131 stairs into Catacombs of Paris at Place Denfert-Rochereau, you'll pass a signpost warning, "Stop! This is the Empire of the Dead." Enter a long tunnel, where you know you will encounter an immense collection of often artfully stacked human bones. Their decorative aspect is highlighted by the purposeful placement of thousands of skulls. Many visitors are undoubtedly caught up in observing these macabre designs and perhaps imagining the lives of those whose remains ended up here. Of course, other visitors are simply there to take a selfie in a most unusual Parisian location. The most fascinating and spooky aspect, however, may be the signage.

At the end of the 18th century, Paris' cemeteries were full. In one case, the weight of thousands of corpses caused the walls of the Holy Innocents cemetery to collapse. The Catacombs was a former underground quarry, where many of the stones were mined for Parisian buildings. It was a convenient place to move millions of bones from cemeteries around the city. Niches in the Catacombs were filled with exhumed skeletons with an outer wall of more decoratively placed bones. In most cases, a stone marker identifies the origin of the bones and the transfer date, starting with the Innocents in 1785. The Catacombs opened to visitors in the early 19th century and continued to add bones for several decades.

Perhaps sensing the future popularity of the Catacombs, identification markers were placed, accompanied by citations, often in both Latin and French, that speak to the fragility of the human condition, the inevitability of death, and the necessity to lead a virtuous life.

*It is sometimes more advantageous to die than to live.*
*I was as you are/You will be as I am.*
*God is not the author of death.*
*The eyes of God are fixed on the just and his ears are open to their prayers.*

Address 1 avenue du Colonel Henri Rol-Tanguy, 75014 Paris, www.catacombes.paris.fr | Getting there Metro to Denfert-Rochereau (Lines 4, 6); RER B to Denfert-Rochereau; bus 38, 59, 68, 88 to Denfert-Rochereau | Hours Tue–Sun 9:45am–8:30pm | Tip The nearby rue Daguerre is a pedestrian-only street with charming shops and restaurants.

# 91 The Paris Mint

*A numismatist's paradise*

In the late 18th century, Louis XV sought to replace a series of ancient mints around the country with a single location in Paris upon which he could stamp his sovereignty. Until 1973, all French coins were minted here, and now the Paris Mint specializes in commemorative coins and other collectibles made in ateliers visible along the museum route. You can even take lessons in metallurgy and technology here.

Look for the tiny, 6th-century B.C. Lydian trite gold coin, the highlight of the exhibit on the various metals used in coinage. Almost every metal – gold, silver, platinum, copper, bronze, tin, nickel, and platinum – has been turned into a coin at some point. If you like old coins with fabulous stories, there are some remarkable collections on display. Don't miss the Treasure of rue Mouffetard, a collection of 3,500 gold coins found in 1938 in the walls of a Parisian building undergoing demolition.

The museum also focuses on the changing technology behind modern coin making. Early coins were labor intensive. A blank was placed between two dies, and a firm strike with a hammer created the finished coin – but you had to hit it just right to get an even imprint. Early 19th-century wheel presses were accurate but still exhausting. In the Industrial Era, steam-powered and later electrified machines could produce many more coins per hour; load up a set of blanks and let the machine do the work. Continuous improvements have made stamping coins easier, quicker, and quieter, leading up to the highly automated, computer-controlled machines of today churning out thousands of shiny, new Euro coins.

After your visit, you can buy coins from the Paris mint boutique honoring French history and culture that cost anywhere from tens to thousands of euros. If you're a recipient of the Legion d'Honneur, this is where you get your medal. It's not your average museum shop.

Address 11 quai de Conti, 75006 Paris, +33 (0)1 40 46 55 00, www.monnaiedeparis.fr | Getting there Bus 27, 58, 70, 87 to Pont Neuf-Quai des Grands Augustins | Hours Tue 11am–6pm, Wed 11am–9pm, Thu–Sun 11am–6pm | Tip The three-Michelin-star restaurant Guy Savoy is located in the same building as the Paris Mint (www.guysavoy.com).

# 92_Paris Sewers Museum

*The city below the city*

The most unlikely museum in Paris is also one of the most fascinating … and fragrant. Located at a collection point along the Seine near the Pont d'Alma, the recently renovated Paris Sewers Museum is a must-visit experience. From here, sewage continues its way to a treatment plant outside Paris while excess rainwater is discharged into the river. You will descend below the street and enter deep inside the city below the city.

The Parisian sewer system is part of the 19th century changes that created today's street grid, brought gas and electrification, and rebuilt housing in the Haussmannian style. You'll quickly realize two things during your visit. First, the sewer system largely mirrors the street grid above. Like roads, the sewer "streets" are of various sizes and named using the same signage as above. You see how pipes bring building wastewater and rainwater directly into the system. Small canals, the *élémentaires,* flow into larger canals, or *collecteurs*, and on to the grand sanitation highways, the *émissaires*. Paris takes advantage of this grid to install water pipes, cables, and other infrastructure. Parts of the old postal pneumatic tube system can be seen in the museum corridors as well.

Second, the museum itself is part of a functioning sewer. The galleries are built above and around actual sewage canals. You will see them, feel their moisture, and smell their contents. Videos and other museum exhibits focus on workers and the equipment they have used to keep the sewage flowing.

Parisians have been visiting the sewers for decades. At one point, it was possible to float down the canals on small tourist boats. Today, guests are a bit more removed from the action. But humans aren't the only visitors. A Nile crocodile named Eleonore was pulled out of a sewer in 1984 and lived for decades in a French zoo. Look for her caricature on one of the museum's walls.

Address Pont de l'Alma, 75007 Paris, +33 (0)1 53 68 27 81, musee-egouts.paris.fr | Getting there Metro to Pont d'Alma (Line 7); RER C to Pont d'Alma; bus 42, 63, 80, 92 to Bosquet-Rapp | Hours Tue–Sun 10am–5pm | Tip A few steps away sits the new Cathédrale de la Sainte-Trinité, the seat of the Russian Orthodox Church, with its spectacular golden onion domes (1 quai Jacques Chirac, cathedrale-sainte-trinite.fr).

# 93 Paul Éluard Museum

*From Carmelite convent to Commune*

The Paul Éluard Museum is known for its unique collections in the city of Saint-Denis. It is also uniquely housed in a cloister for Carmelite nuns during the 17th century. Madame Louise, the daughter of Louis XV, resided here too. Your visit will take you through the Carmelite convent, the gardens, the 1779 chapel, rooms dedicated to archeology, an 18th-century apothecary, and landscapes by Paul Signac and Jean-Baptiste-Camille Corot. But two bodies of work here are particularly famous, thanks to their originality, scope, and diversity: the Paris Commune Collection and the Paul Éluard Collection.

The Paris Commune (1871), the last French Revolution, is a period of history that is not very well known. This collection, the most comprehensive in existence, includes works of art, posters, objects, and newspapers that recount the story of this attempt at a social revolution. A highlight is a large shadow box about the annus horribilis illustrating the atrocities committed during the siege. Nicolas Kohl, a carriage painter, collected the objects inside this glass case, which serve as poignant reminders of the violence of that era: a piece of coal found in the remains of a person during the bloody week, and the bones of a rat or cat that had been eaten by something – or someone.

The Paul Éluard Fund, on the other hand, was a gift from the poet to his native city in 1951. It includes a set of artworks and manuscripts that reflect Éluard's poetic genius, his love of art, and his surrealist and political engagements. The gem of the collection is the first draft of the poem *Liberty* (1941). Initially a love poem dedicated to Éluard's wife, it would later evolve into a powerful statement during the Resistance movement. French children still learn it in school. It was revived in all its political force after the 2015 terrorist attacks to voice support for the victims.

Address 22 bis rue Gabriel Péri, 93200 Saint-Denis, +33 (0)1 83 72 24 55, www.musee-saint-denis.fr/, musee@ville-saint-denis.fr | Getting there Metro to Port de Paris (Line 13); RER D to Gare de Saint-Denis; tramway T1 to Basilique de Saint Denis, T5 to Marché de Saint-Denis; bus 154 to Gare de Saint-Denis, 153, 170 to Porte de Paris | Hours Mon, Wed, Fri 10am–5:30pm, Thu 10am–8pm, Sat & Sun 2–6:30pm | Tip The last battles of the Paris Commune were concentrated in Père-Lachaise Cemetery, where nearly 200 Communards were shot against the wall in a northeastern section. A marble plaque there reads, "To the dead of the Commune, May 21–28, 1871" (16 Rue du Repos, www.paris.fr).

# 94 Petit Palais

*Realist masterpieces in a Beaux-Arts icon*

The Petit Palais was initially built to introduce the world to French art at the 1900 Universal Exhibition. It is now the City of Paris' museum of fine arts, featuring works from antiquity to the 19th century. The museum displays an eclectic range of paintings, sculptures, and furniture. The collections at the Petit Palais are wide-ranging, although it is known predominantly as a 19th-century museum.

Galleries devoted to the 19th century show the rise of naturalism, starting with Gustave Courbet. Among the notable works is *Le Sommeil*, a daring canvas portraying two intertwined naked women. The painting was commissioned by a Turkish diplomat intrigued by Courbet's portrayal of women, and it provoked considerable scandal.

Realism finds an extension through the works of naturalist painters as they strived to depict urban life and the working-class communities. The City of Paris supported this movement through its purchases. In 1889, Léon Lhermitte painted a monumental work for the Paris City Hall. *L'approvisionnement des Halles*, depicting Paris' historic food market, caused a sensation at the 1895 Salon and elicited numerous comments. While some criticized its subject matter as trivial, everyone recognized the vitality of the scene and the painter's virtuosity. In 1904, the artwork found its home in the Petit Palais but was later stored, rolled up in reserve until 2013.

In contrast, Fernand Pelez chose to devote himself to capturing the lives of the humble and destitute. His somber painting *La parade des humbles* is a critical depiction of circus performers, portraying the circus as a joyless affair of fatigue and tired tricks. These canvases represent the Paris of Émile Zola, and for a long time they were overlooked and forgotten. Recognizing their significance, the Petit Palais has rightfully brought these brilliant works back into the public eye.

**Address** Avenue Winston-Churchill, 75008 Paris, +33 (0)1 53 43 40 00, www.petitpalais.paris.fr | **Getting there** Metro to Champs-Élysées-Clemenceau (Lines 1, 13); bus 42, 73 to Champs-Élysées-Clemenceau, 72, 93 to Grand Palais | **Hours** Tue–Sun 10am–6pm | **Tip** The Hôtel de la Païva is listed as a historic monument as a rare example of decorative arts under the Second Empire. Tours are available by reservation (25 Avenue des Champs Élysées, www.paris-capitale-historique.fr/visite/hotel-paiva).

# 95_Phono Museum Paris

*Bringing old music and technology back to life*

As it turns out, Thomas Edison and Gustave Eiffel, two great innovators of the 19th century, were admirers of each other. This is one of the things you will learn while visiting the Phono Museum Paris.

Edison was in Paris in August 1889 for the Universal Exposition to demonstrate his phonograph, which both recorded and replayed sound on wax cylinders. During the exposition, he rode to the top of the Eiffel Tower with Native American members of Buffalo Bill's Wild West show. Later, Gustave Eiffel held a luncheon for Edison, who demonstrated his phonograph in Eiffel's private apartment at the top of the tower. At Phono Museum Paris, you can listen to the 1889 Edison phonograph, which was also famous for being powered by electricity, the other star of the Exposition.

In addition to this Edison model, the museum offers a remarkable collection of phonographs that spans their entire history. These include the 1878 Tinfoil phonograph, which is the earliest example of a machine that recorded sound on foil for a single playback.

The museum also boasts rare 1880s models from Alexander Graham Bell, many other models of Edison phonographs, and the machines of Emile Berliner, who created the term "gramophone" and led the transition from wax cylinders to flat discs. The history of Victor Records is told through a series of phonographs and an original painting of the famous Victor Records dog. French innovation is represented by several phonographs from the Pathé brothers, including a large dance hall model constructed inside a beautiful art nouveau case.

Phono Museum Paris is absolutely stuffed with the history of recorded sound. The staff will provide expert knowledge of every phonograph, and, best of all, they'll play music for you on almost all of them. As the museum's founder Jalal Aro says, "The most extraordinary machines are those we can make play again."

**Address** 53 boulevard de Rochechouart, 75009 Paris, +33 (0)1 80 61 59 37, phonomuseum.fr, phonomp@gmail.com | **Getting there** Metro to Anvers (Line 2) or Pigalle (Line 12); bus 54 to Rochechouart-Martyrs | **Hours** Fri & Sun 10am–6pm, Mon–Thu & Sat 9am–6pm by appointment | **Tip** You can peer through the windows of Eiffel's secret apartment at the top of the Eiffel Tower and see the figures of Eiffel and Edison and his original phonograph (Champ de Mars, 7 avenue Anatole, www.toureiffel.paris).

# 96 Picasso National Museum

*The venerated giant of modern art*

The Picasso National Museum is located in the Hôtel Salé, one of the Marais' finest private mansions. It features the most important collection of works by Spanish painter and sculptor Pablo Picasso (1881–1973), the giant of modern art. This collection stands out for its exceptional quality, breadth, and diversity, encompassing paintings, engravings, ceramics, graphic arts, drawings, and sculptures. It is the sole public collection that offers a comprehensive overview of the artist's career. The museum also showcases Picasso's personal collection of African art and works by his contemporaries. You'll grasp the artist's genius through the semi-permanent chronological or thematic displays. The museum also organizes temporary exhibitions of contemporary artists whose work resonates with that of Picasso.

Throughout his career, Picasso was profoundly influenced by the women in his life: Fernande Olivier, Dora Maar, Eva Gouel, Olga Khokhlova, Marie-Thérèse Walter, and the others. He maintained relationships with them that were both inspiring and passionate. 1932 was a pivotal year in Picasso's life, as he was celebrated with a retrospective exhibition at the Georges Petit Gallery. Picasso was 50 years old then and quite famous. Married to Olga for 15 years, the artist would sneak away to join Marie-Thérèse, his 23-year-old mistress, whom he would paint frantically in his Parisian studio. She was the muse who inspired some of his most acclaimed paintings, including *Le Rêve*.

After he met Marie-Thérèse, Picasso debuted a new pictorial language. He depicted her using simplified shapes and rounded volumes with her distinctive features of blonde hair and round breasts. Picasso juxtaposed viewpoints to create a new perspective, while alternating hues of purple, green, red, and yellow created depth and dimension to the overlapping volumes. A sense of sensuality and tenderness emerge from this work.

Address 5 rue de Thorigny, 75003 Paris, +33 (0)1 85 56 00 36, www.museepicassoparis.fr | Getting there Métro to Saint Paul (Line 1), Saint-Sébastien Froissard or Chemin Vert (Line 8); bus 29 to Vieille du Temple, 67, 69, 72, 76, 96 to Vieille du Temple-Mairie du 4e | Hours Tue–Sun 9:30am–6pm | Tip Take a short detour to visit the oldest food market in the capital, The Enfants Rouges covered market. Stock up on fresh produce and enjoy a lunch break at the Italian grocery store, Lebanese caterer, or Japanese snack bar (39 rue de Bretagne, www.parisinfo.com/shopping-paris).

# 97 Poincaré House

*Where math comes to life*

Nestled within the campus of the Henri Poincaré Institute (IHP) and next to the Curie Museum, is one of Paris' newest museums. The Maison Poincaré is installed in several former research spaces, including the former office of Nobel Prize-winning physicist Jean Baptiste Perrin. Here, you'll explore the many concepts and facets of mathematics through a series of informative displays, games, video, and even mixed-reality experiences.

The interactive games in the "Modeling" gallery explain fundamental math concepts. Flip a virtual coin 50 times to learn about the concept of probability, or play the role of a Border collie to experience the algorithms involved in herding sheep. In a former teaching amphitheater, the "Inventing" gallery features a video that explores how mathematicians work together to make new discoveries, and several interviews enthusiastically recount moments of invention. The most fascinating aspect of the "Sharing" gallery is the examples of physical representations of mathematical models. Constructed from many different materials, these objects constitute the IHP's collection of fine art. In the "Visualizing" space, participants don a helmet and enter the virtual world of 3D shapes representing the results of mathematical calculations. It's a fascinating journey, and the effect is a room full of people chasing virtual objects through space.

The most important exhibit may be in the "Becoming" gallery, particularly for school groups. You are invited to explore your own preconceptions about who mathematicians are in the life-sized presence of Dr. Perrin, himself an older white Frenchman. But you'll also see the photos of current mathematicians of every gender, national origin, and ethnicity displayed on the room's walls. Students who are 13 or 14 years old and trying to map out their futures are encouraged to imagine themselves as a part of this world.

Address 11 rue Pierre et Marie Curie, 75005 Paris, +33 (0)1 44 27 64 73, www.ihp.fr/en/outreach, info-maison-poincare@ihp.fr | Getting there Metro to Cardinal Lemoine (Line 10), Place Monge (Line 7); RER B to Luxembourg; bus 24 to Musée et Institut Curie, 21, 27 to Saint-Jacques – Guy-Lussac | Hours Mon & Tue, Thu & Fri 8:30am – 6pm, Sat 10am – 6pm | Tip The neighborhood from the Institute to the Pantheon features small murals of Pierre and Marie Curie, resistance fighter Berty Albrecht, chemist Marcellin Berthelot, and philosophers Denis Diderot and Henri Bergson.

# 98 Police Museum

*More than just the guillotine*

The guillotine is a lasting symbol of the French Revolution, but did you know that it remained a method for execution of criminals sentenced to death in France until 1977? This is one of the many surprising things you'll learn on a visit to the Police Museum.

This small but very comprehensive museum covers the period from the 17th century, when there were competing groups performing a variety of city administration duties, through to the establishment of a formal police force by Napoleon in 1800, and up to the present day. The museum highlights the evolution of policing and trends in criminality. A period of anarchist terrorism and gang violence in the late 19th century changed police organization and the available tools. Foot patrols and nightsticks gave way to police cars and Browning pistols.

In 1914, the first policing school was established to teach investigative methods and ethical practices. A display on the "morals police" highlights the changing attitudes toward prostitution. Moving on to the 20th century, the museum includes a small memorial to the 167 policemen who were killed fighting for the liberation of Paris.

The French police force has also played a critical role in the development of technologies for combatting crime and recidivism. In 1882, after noticing that false identities made it harder to track criminals, Alphonse Bertillon developed a new method to identify possible repeat offenders through the recording of 14 physical measurements, including height and head size. He also introduced the practice of taking head-on and side-view mug shots as illustrated by the museum's recreation of his studio. The police took up to 100 sets of measurements per week and soon had records of thousands of convicted criminals and possible suspects. This system was used for many years until it was replaced by fingerprinting and other, newer technologies.

Address 4 rue de la Montagne Sainte-Geneviève, 75005 Paris, +33 (0)1 44 41 52 50, www.prefecturedepolice.interieur.gouv.fr/musee# | Getting there Metro to Maubert-Mutualité (Line 10); bus 24, 47, 63, 86, 87 to Maubert-Mutualité | Hours Tue–Wed, Fri 9:30am–5pm; Thu 9:30am–7pm; 1st & 3rd Sat 10:30am–5:30pm | Tip La Maison d'Isabelle around the corner on Place Maubert has received awards for its incredible croissants, and its baguettes and palmiers are mouthwatering too (47ter boulevard Saint Germain).

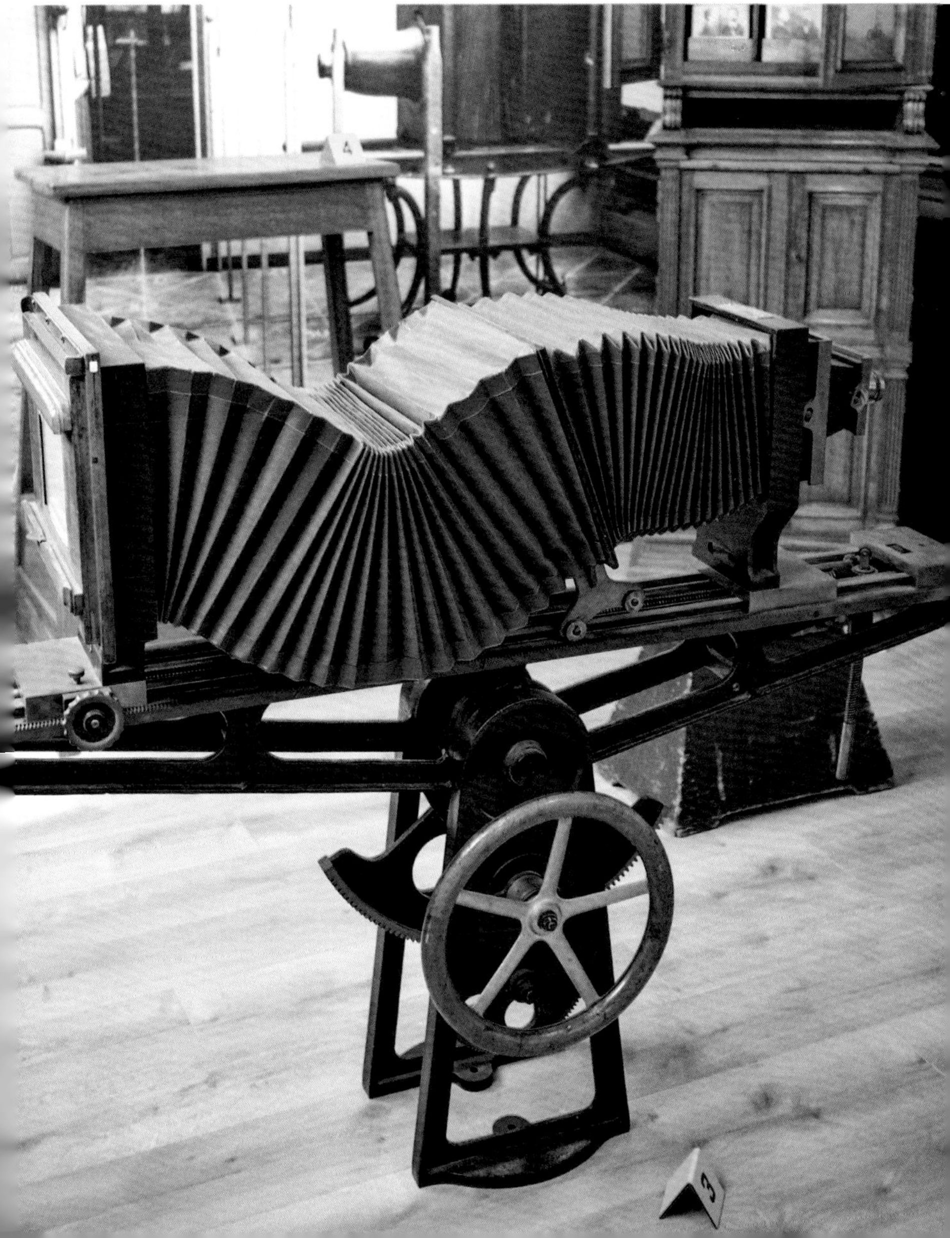

# 99 The Pompidou Center

*The heart of modern and contemporary art*

The Centre Georges Pompidou is instantly recognizable by its floating architecture and colorful pipes. Its dynamic appeal lies in the breadth of its collections of more than 120,000 works and in its temporary exhibitions covering a wide range of significant movements in modern and contemporary art worldwide. Thanks to its rich reserves, the museum updates its spaces every eight months in an ongoing invitation to discover new facets of art.

Whether you are a modern art connoisseur or a casual observer, the exhibition halls take you on a journey connecting the museum's two permanent collections, namely Modern and Contemporary Art. Starting with Modern Art (1905 – 1950) on level 5, works are displayed chronologically so you can follow the evolution of modern artistic thought. The collection begins with Fauvism, an early 20th-century movement that introduced distortion in representations of reality. Step by step, the collection moves away from faithful representations toward other centers of interest, such as color and shape. You will witness the emergence of artistic movements that revolutionized one's very perception of a painting. Smaller galleries complete the journey, highlighting the critical role played by art dealers in championing the recognition of contemporary artists.

On level 4, the Contemporary Art section, anything is possible. You'll see the works of established artists as well as emerging talents. Here, you can expect to encounter artworks that evoke confusion, provoke contemplation, or trigger emotions.

The essence of contemporary art is to challenge our preconceived notions. Whether it is a room filled with dried bay leaves or a stroll through a forest of headphones, the art here aims to surprise and engage you, the viewer, sparking questions and inviting you to view the world from many fresh perspectives.

Address 1 place Georges Pompidou, 75004 Paris, +33 (0)1 44 78 12 33, www.centrepompidou.fr | Getting there Metro to Rambuteau (Line 11), Hôtel de Ville (Lines 1, 11), Chatelet (Lines 1, 4, 7, 11, 14); RER A, B, D to Chatelet–Les Halles; bus 28, 75 to Centre Georges Pompidou | Hours Mon–Wed & Fri–Sun 11am–9pm, Thu 11am–11pm | Tip Four minutes from the Pompidou Center, you can relax in Anne Frank Garden, a small oasis of greenery (14 Impasse Berthaud, www.parisinfo.com/musee-monument-paris/71173/Jardin-Anne-Frank).

# 100 Postal Museum

*Did you get my letter?*

The postal service is an everyday part of our lives and something that we often take for granted. The new postal museum, masterfully renovated and reopened in 2019 as a series of open and inviting spaces, is a brilliant example of using stories and artifacts to assert the ongoing importance of a longtime institution. The museum's many exhibits include historical collections of uniforms, postboxes, sacks, and signage, as well as a display of every French stamp issued since 1849.

The museum's exhibits highlight the evolving methods of postal delivery. True postal services started in the 16th century with *la poste aux chevaux*, or pony express. An early 19th-century postal rider's uniform includes an enormous pair of black iron boots. Designed to protect the rider's legs, each boot weighed almost 3 kilograms (7 pounds), and they could not be used for walking.

Throughout the 18th and 19th centuries, a series of horse-driven coaches and messengers reduced delivery times between major cities. As technology advanced, the combination of mobile postal bureaus and faster transport times made the postal service one of the first users of the train in 1841, through to 2015. To improve mail delivery to rural areas, the postal service began using special Renault postal vehicles in 1926. This special service ended in 1990, but trucks still transport most French mail today. Given France's fascination with flight, it's natural that air service started in 1912, not long after Louis Bleriot's flight across the English Channel.

One of the biggest surprises in the postal museum is the exhibit of the pneumatic machine. Did you know that, starting in 1866 and installed in the sewer tunnels, a 450-kilometer (280-mile) pneumatic tube network once connected 130 Parisian post offices? It circulated millions of pieces of mail until newer technologies forced it to cease operation in 1984.

Address 34 boulevard de Vaugirard, 75015 Paris, +33 (0)1 42 79 24 24, www.museedelaposte.fr, museeposte.info@laposte.fr | **Getting there** Metro to Pasteur (Lines 6, 12), Montparnasse-Bienvenüe (Lines 4, 6, 12, 13); bus 39, 91, 95 to Armorique-Musée Postal | **Hours** Wed–Mon 11am–6pm | **Tip** A visit to the *Marché aux timbres,* or Stamp Market, is a must for the budding philatelist (corner of avenue Marigny and avenue Gabriel, www.parisinfo. com/shopping/73776/Marche-aux-timbres).

# 101_Quai Branly-Jacques Chirac Museum

*Journey to the far reaches of the world*

The Quai Branly-Jacques Chirac Museum puts indigenous art in the spotlight with exhibits focusing on Asia, Africa, Oceania, and the Americas. The museum resides in an innovative building resting on stilts, designed by architect Jean Nouvel. You're in for a captivating immersion into civilizations that may be unfamiliar. The 3,500 works representing only one percent of the museum's collection are displayed by geographical area and continuously change.

Of all the continents, Oceania remains the most elusive. It covers vast territories and a multitude of archipelagos and atolls. The artistic expressions found in this region demonstrate immense diversity and reveal the profound connections that bind people to their environment, their ways of life, and their beliefs. The Bisj poles are a striking example of this idea. These majestic sculptured poles adorned with motifs were created by the Asmat people from the island of New Guinea.

As local myths recount, the souls of the deceased find peace in the realm of the spirits. But before reaching their final destination, souls can wander, cause trouble, or even upset the balance of the community. Bisj poles serve as a reminder of the deaths of villagers and encourage headhunting raids against an enemy village to avenge the dead and guide the souls to peace. The aim of this practice is to keep the group balanced and ensure fertility and security. After the headhunting expeditions, a traditional ceremony is held, where men recite the names of their headhunting victims. When they have finished, the poles are returned to the mangrove, where they will rot and fertilize the sago palms. The cycle of life and death is thus respected. A trip to Quai Branly lets you unravel the mysteries of these remote civilizations.

**Address** 37 quai Branly, 75007 Paris, +33 (0)1 56 61 70 00, www.quaibranly.fr | **Getting there** Metro to Alma-Marceau (Line 9), École Militaire (Line 8); RER C to Pont de l'Alma; bus 42 to Tour Eiffel, 63, 80, 92 to Bosquet-Rapp, 69 to Champ de Mars, 72 to Musée d'Art Moderne-Palais de Tokyo, 82 to Varsovie, 87 to Rapp-La Bourdonnais | **Hours** Tue & Wed, Fri–Sun 10:30am–7pm, Thu 10:30am–10pm | **Tip** Take time to walk through Gilles Clément's lush, 4.5 acre (1.8-hectare) garden with 15,000 hand-selected plant species. And don't miss the enormous green wall designed by the botanist Patrick Blanc (http://www.greenroofs.com/projects/musee-du-quai-branly-greenwall).

# 102 Rodin Museum

*Assembled masterpieces*

The Rodin Museum is one of the rare museums created by the artist himself, and so it has both a soul and an artistic imprint. At the end of his career, Auguste Rodin (1840–1917) moved to the Hôtel Biron, a space rented by artists. Enamored with the light in this space, Rodin sought to preserve it for posterity. With government support, he was able to turn the mansion into a museum. At the Rodin Museum, you have the unique opportunity to view the artist's works and understand his creative process. You'll discover the various stages of crafting sculptures through the display of drawings and plaster models. It feels a bit as if you are sitting next to Rodin himself, watching him at work.

The galleries devoted to artworks from the later phase of his career are surprising. This is a lesser-known Rodin. He no longer has anything to prove but continues his research, driven by a passion for antiquity and foreign civilizations. Rodin compiled a repertoire of forms as he recognized that the fragmented state of certain works did not alter their beauty. He was one of the first sculptors to represent individual body parts and sought out new realms of shapes, joyfully assembling fragments and playing with proportions. Prepare yourself to be surprised as you can admire a woman who seems to be taking a bath in a teacup, a bust of a man emerging from a vase, and pieces of intertwined limbs. It is radical for its time and completely off beat. The end of Rodin's career reflects his creative freedom.

Make sure to spend time with the works that contributed to Rodin's fame: *The Kiss*, *The Thinker*, *The Cathedral*, *Balzac*. Rodin delighted in juxtaposing extremes, blending subtlety and sensuality with expressions of anguish and pain. The power of expression in his sculptures is exceptional, and you are certain to find a work that resonates with your own emotions and experiences.

Address 77 rue de Varenne, 75007 Paris, +33 (0)1 44 18 61 10, www.musee-rodin.fr | Getting there Metro to Varenne (Line 13), Invalides (Lines 8, 13); bus 69, 83, 87, 92 to Invalides | Hours Tue–Sun 10am–6:30pm | Tip Many Rodin statues can be found throughout Paris, including the *Statue de d'Alembert* on the left corner of the Hôtel de Ville façade (5 rue de Lobau), the bas-relief on the façade of the former Théâtre des Gobelins (73 avenue des Gobelins), and on the façade of the Hôtel de la Païva (25 avenue des Champs Elysées).

# 103 Rodin Museum Meudon

*Daily life within the master's home*

Auguste Rodin (1840–1917) bought this home after his breakup with Camille Claudel. Cows and horses roamed the grounds, and there were cabins for his workers. His studio of antiquities adjoined the main house, which is quite modest, while the property looks like a small village. This was a place where Rodin could work and invite guests. In the lower part of the garden, Rodin installed the Pavillon de L'Alma, a structure commissioned in Paris in 1900 for the artist's first solo exhibition. It would become his enormous, light-filled studio. Rodin and his wife Rose Beuret are buried beside the studio beneath *The Thinker*.

Rodin's studio displays his works in plaster, his working medium. Shapes were molded and stored as he worked through a process of assembly. Look for the different iterations of Victor Hugo – dressed, naked, with no arms or arms outstretched, with or without muses, and the final armless version. Rodin engaged in a perpetual process of tinkering, where the aesthetic result mattered less to him than the form itself. He was deliberate and took his time, as evidenced by the ten years he took to complete his sculpture of *The Burghers of Calais*.

After receiving approval for a model of the piece, he was unsatisfied with his work and made changes. The version that was approved had featured a triumphant arm raised forward, but upon further reflection, Rodin thought, "The bourgeois are experiencing a time of terrible fear. I want to represent fear, dread, human misery." So he created another version that was rejected. This is the story of Rodin and the artist's freedom to venture beyond an era's conventions and concentrate on communicating emotions.

Critics of the time lauded Rodin as the artist who breathed life into sculpture. Rodin's primary interest lay in delving into the realm of emotion and exploring the boundless capacity for expression.

Address 19 avenue Auguste Rodin, 92190 Meudon, +33 (0)1 41 14 35 00, www.meudon.musee-rodin.fr | Getting there Metro to Mairie d'Issy (Line 12); RER C to Meudon-Val-Fleury then bus 190, 290, 169 to Hôpital Percy | Hours Mar–Oct, Sat & Sun 10am–6pm | Tip You are encouraged to picnic on the grounds of the property, but remember to bring your own picnic basket, as there are no restaurants or refreshments on the premises or in the immediate neighborhood.

# 104_Sèvres Museum

*The first museum devoted entirely to ceramics*

The Sèvres Museum dedicated to ceramic arts was founded in 1824 by Alexandre Brongniart, then director of the Sèvres Manufacture. Brongniart envisioned the creation of a museum displaying ceramic pieces from around the world. The goal was to provide his craftsmen with inspiration and give them the means to improve their techniques. The museum has continued to expand, and today it holds a collection of 50,000 pieces from every period and country. Ceramics have many more uses than simply tableware. Your visit here will be filled with surprises.

The collection encompasses an array of magnificent works, including ancient works, ceramics from Iznik in Turkey and the Middle East, Chinese porcelain, Italian Renaissance majolica, Medici and Delft ceramics, pre-Columbian terracotta from South America, and pieces from European and French manufacturers. You will discover that China's influence on the world of ceramics has been profound since it was the first country to develop the techniques for porcelain in the 7th century. Europe would unravel the mystery centuries later. Several rooms are dedicated to the collections of Sèvres porcelain, revealing the combination of Italian Renaissance majolica and Chinese porcelain that influenced the factory. The 18th-century artist François Boucher, who held the title of First Painter to the King, revitalized Sèvres with a style that gained recognition worldwide.

Sèvres porcelain is characterized by its celestial blue color, and for a long period, it was the sole company capable of skillfully applying gold to porcelain. Esteemed artists spanning various eras have created remarkable works in Sèvres porcelain, including Boucher and Rodin, and contemporary artists Louise Bourgeois and Ettore Sottsass.

Notable highlights of the collection include the Etruscan vase commissioned by Napoleon and the impressive, towering, 3.15-meter (10.3-foot) Neptune vase.

**Address** 2 place de la Manufacture, 92310 Sèvres, +33 (0)1 46 29 22 05, www.sevresciteceramique.fr, visite@sevresciteceramique.fr | **Getting there** Metro to Pont de Sèvres (Line 9); tramway 2 to Musée de Sèvres; bus 169, 171, 179, 426 to Musée de Sèvres | **Hours** Mon, Wed–Fri 10am–1pm & 2–6pm, Sat & Sun 10am–6pm | **Tip** You can visit the workshops at the Sèvres factory by reservation and see their remarkable processes firsthand (2 place de la Manufacture, sèvrevisite@sevresciteceramique.fr).

# 105 Shoah Memorial

*Bearing witness to the Holocaust*

In a world of deepening division, rising anti-Semitism, Holocaust denial, and ignorance about the Holocaust among younger generations, the work of the Shoah Memorial and related museums is more important than ever.

In 1943, the Contemporary Jewish Documentation Center (CDJC) began to collect evidence of persecution. As France neared liberation, the CDJC took control of the records of the German Army, embassy, and the Gestapo, and the Vichy Government. Those records were used by prosecutors at Nuremburg and later trials. To this day, the memorial's central goal is to document, to bear witness, and to educate visitors about the Holocaust. In addition to the names of French Jews who died during the war, the memorial maintains a Wall of the Righteous Among the Nations, a list of non-Jews who risked their own safety to save Jews in France.

The permanent exhibition here tells the story of Jews in Europe and France through official records, pictures, artifacts, and videos. It begins with a map showing the size of European Jewish populations in 1929 alongside a description of pre-war Jewish society and historical antisemitism. With themes such as "The Rise of Nazism," "From Exclusion to the First Camps," "The Extermination Camps," "The Plunder of Jews in France," and "Resistance," the exhibition documents the increasingly dire situation for French Jews from the 1930s and their fight for survival. Video accounts of survivors such as Simone Weil attach history to real people.

It can be painful and possibly even numbing to learn about such brutality. Perhaps this explains why the memorial has chosen to end the exhibition with a brightly lit room full of photos of children deported from France. It is impossible not to be moved or to forget once you are faced with the death of the Asz sisters, the Perel twins, or the five young siblings of the Waks family.

Address 17 rue Geoffroy l'Asnier, 75004 Paris, +33 (0)1 42 77 44 72, www.memorialdelashoah.org, contact@memorialdelashoah.org | Getting there Metro to Pont Marie (Line 7), Saint-Paul (Line 1); bus 67, 72 to Pont Marie | Hours Mon–Wed 10am–6pm, Thu 10am–10pm, Fri & Sun 10am–6pm | Tip The Mémorial des Martyrs de la Déportation sits on the site of a former morgue near Notre Dame Cathedral and remembers those deported by Vichy France to Nazi concentration camps (7 Quai de l'Archevêché, www.onac-vg.fr).

# 106 Smoking Museum

*Smoking when it was better ...*

Not every museum in Paris is a grand art institution. A neighborhood smoke shop houses one of the smaller museums in the city. Behind the shop's front counter, with its tobacco and vape products, sits the Museum of Smoking. It comprises display cabinets, a hallway, and the shop's bathroom. In that space, the owners have created an exhibition of historical artifacts and smoking paraphernalia, including several extraordinary pieces.

The museum tells the tale of several hundred years of smoking through documentation, illustrations, caricatures, and various smoking instruments. A small exhibit focuses on the role of smoking in women's liberation told through the stories of geishas and George Sand. Dozens of satirical and historical prints illustrate the importance of smoking in 18th- and 19th-century society. There are bongs, hookahs, clay and hemp pipes, western wood pipes and carved meerschaums, and the specialized pipes used for opium. 20th-century items include early cigarette packs, rolling paper, and amusing little figurines used to store matchsticks.

The most compelling exhibit is a North American Indian peace pipe. Peace pipes were used in religious ceremonies and to seal treaties and other agreements. Long and slender, the pipe is decorated with a wrap of fringed leather and red, white and blue beadwork, and it is the museum's most prized possession and an unexpected find in Paris.

Near the back of the shop, the small bathroom, or "Portrait Room," houses one more curious exhibit. Along with a larger portrait of Serge Gainsbourg, hundreds of small framed pictures of celebrities smoking, including Jimmy Hendrix, Marlene Dietrich, and Brigitte Bardot, line the walls of the bathroom. Although smoking is in decline throughout much of the world, this exhibit reminds you just how deeply it has been embedded in French and global popular culture.

Address 7 rue Pache, 75011 Paris, +33 (0)1 46 59 05 51, www.museedufumeur.net, info@museedufumeur.net | Getting there Metro to Voltaire (Line 9); bus 46, 56, 61, 69 to Place Léon Blum | Hours Mon–Sat noon–7:30pm | Tip La Briée nearby specializes in many types of brioche from the classic buttery Parisian variety to the pink praline of Lyon to Alsatian almond kouglof (69 rue Sedaine, www.labriee.com).

# 107 Trade Guild Museum

*French know-how and excellence*

French craftsmanship embodies the art of living and luxury, and it is a testament to French history. *Compagnonnage* is a centuries-old tradition and a guarantee of know-how and French excellence. However, it is largely unknown. The *compagnons*, or tradespeople, are the heirs of the great builders of French cathedrals. The Trade Guild Museum, located in the former headquarters of the Compagnons Charpentier du Devoir de Liberté in the 6th arrondissement, offers an immersive experience of this mysterious world. The highlight of the visit is a volunteer compagnon, who will introduce you to the museum's treasures and reveal the secrets of this guild.

In 2010, *Compagnonnage* was recognized by UNESCO and included on the Representative List of Intangible Cultural Heritage. The essence of *compagnonnage* is to provide vocational training and life skills to young people after their apprenticeships in a manual trade, such as carpentry. The roots of this tradition are unclear, but it is believed to have emerged from trade associations that began organizing in the 13th century.

*Compagnonnage* gradually started appearing in the 15th century, evolving and diversifying according to each trade by the end of the 17th century. *Compagnonnage* is defined by its values, the constant pursuit of improvement, travel throughout France, customs, symbols, rites, and legends. The *compagnons* call these values their "duty." During your visit to this small museum, you'll discover fine craftsmanship and tools, most of which will be a complete mystery to you. Luckily, a *compagnon* will provide explanations. Photographs from the post-war period bear witness to their traditions, including pictures of pieces exhibited on the street by *compagnons* as part of craftsmanship contests. However, the most fascinating aspect lies in learning about the journey and passion of the *compagnons* themselves.

Address 10 rue Mabillon, 75006 Paris, +33 (0)1 43 26 25 03 | Getting there Metro to Mabillon (Line 9); bus 63, 86, 87, 70, 96 to Seine-Buci | Hours Tue & Fri 2–6pm | Tip Aux Arts et Sciences Réunis is the restaurant of the carpenter *compagnons*. One room houses monumental masterpieces from the 19th century (161 avenue Jean Jaurès, www.aux-arts-et-sciences-reunis.fr).

# 108_ Victor Hugo House

*Much more than a genius writer*

Victor Hugo House pays tribute to the renowned writer by displaying different periods of his life through decorative experiments. A fascinating and complex person, Hugo was passionate about so much more than writing.

He was at the same time a decorator, cartoonist, humanist, and politician. The tour of the house offers glimpses into his passions for decoration, drawing, and learning, making it a place of enjoyment, enlightenment – and even a touch of whimsy.

Victor Hugo lived in this apartment from 1832 to 1848, but his passion for décor flourished during his 18 years in exile in Guernsey. He had an affinity for antiques, loved the thrill of bargain hunting, and had a passion for all things Gothic. He bought armoires, chests, and tables. He enjoyed disassembling them and repurposing them, diverting them from their original functions. A door would become a table, while his desk was assembled from different pieces of furniture. His creations highlight human freedom and ingenuity. For him, décor and design had a deep commemorative significance. His son Charles said of him, "Victor Hugo's writing and thoughts may be directed at the present, but his artistic tastes are turned to the past."

A unique artifact is the little bird mirror, which reflects the many facets of his personality. Here is Victor Hugo the designer, decorator, poet, grandfather, and politician. He crafted the mirror for his lover Juliette Drouet during a tumultuous moment in his life when he was convicted in absentia for voting against Napoleon III's referendum. On the mirror, Victor Hugo drew a wooden fence, flowers, leaves, and birds. He added a poem dedicated to his grandson Little George. The drawing represents the small fence that he had built around a fountain to prevent his grandson from falling into the water. This mirror is full of tenderness and love.

**Address** 6 place des Vosges, 75004 Paris, +33 (0)1 42 72 10 16, www.maisonsvictorhugo.paris.fr | **Getting there** Metro to Saint-Paul (Line 1), Bastille (Lines 1, 5, 8) , Chemin Vert (Line 8); bus (29, 96) to Place des Vosges | **Hours** Tue–Sun 10am–6pm | **Tip** Looking for books from France's rich literary heritage? There are many to choose from at the bookshop in the Hôtel Sully (62 rue Saint Antoine).

# 109 Wine Museum

*Wine caves and Balzac's escape*

It is fitting that the world's premier winemaking country has a museum dedicated to wine in its capital. Paris and its environs, particularly the commune of Argentueil, was the largest viniculture region in France for several hundred years. The Wine Museum itself is located in the Passy neighborhood, where limestone quarries once supplied stone for the city's construction. The monastery of the Order of Minims stood on the site surrounded by terraced gardens and vineyards from 1472 until the Revolution. The brothers produced one of Louis XIII's favorite wines, and their wine cellars were cut into the limestone walls. The cellars are now occupied by the museum's galleries.

The Council of Echansons of France, established to maintain the knowledge and quality of French wine and to promote its appellations, has operated the museum since 1984. Visitors will learn the history of winemaking and see the techniques and tools used by winemakers. The winding cellars house a collection of thousands of artifacts – extending back to pottery of the Gallo-Roman era – that are used to explain different aspects of the winemaking process. You'll be surprised to learn how many tools go into the care of vines, fermenting of grapes, and bottling of wine. These tools include hoes and ploughs, copper stills, and a vast collection of bottles. While you might have one or two corkscrews, a traditional model and a modern one that eases uncorking, the museum's collection is comparatively vast.

Wax figures of coopers and champagne makers, plus famous figures like Napoleon and Louis Pasteur, further illustrate France's rich wine history. Look for the writer (and coffeeholic) Honoré de Balzac entering the cellars from a secret stairwell coming from the streets above. Balzac used it to hide from the tax collectors.

Finally, don't forget to enjoy a glass of wine at the end of your visit.

Address 5 square Charles Dickens, 75016 Paris, +33 (0)1 45 25 63 26, www.lemparis.com, info@museeduvinparis.com | Getting there Metro to Passy (Line 6); bus 32 to Passy-La Tour, 72 to Pont de Bir-Hakeim | Hours Tue–Sat 10am–6pm | Tip There are ten vineyards inside Paris, including 700 pinot noir vines in Parc Georges Brassens (2 place Jacques Marette).

# 110_Yves Saint Laurent Museum

*The grand collection of an iconic designer*

The Yves Saint Laurent Museum pays tribute to the creations of one of the most iconic couturiers of the 20th century. Yves Saint Laurent (1936–2008) is the only designer of his generation to have archived all his work starting the moment his fashion house was created, thanks to the Pierre Bergé-Yves Saint Laurent Foundation. Since the 1960s, the foundation has assembled more than 7,000 haute couture creations, which are exhibited in rotation.

The museum is situated within the historic premises of the renowned Yves Saint Laurent haute couture house in a private mansion from the Second Empire era. Saint Laurent worked there for nearly three decades from 1974 to 2002. The studio constitutes the heart of your visit as the museum's true nerve center, where the designer meticulously conceived every creation with his team. The studio has been reconstructed faithfully: his glasses resting on his desk, his pencils, a photograph of Catherine Deneuve, and his drawings that appear as though they were sketched just moments ago. It feels as if Yves Saint Laurent could stride into his office at any moment.

The museum traces the designer's career, including sketches made when he was only 15 years old. One room is dedicated to his creative process, with sketches, notebooks, and annotations, all essential elements of his upstream work before bringing his designs to life. The exhibition then transitions to his iconic haute couture collections, including the revolutionary women's tuxedo, the timeless trench coat, the safari jacket, and the little black dress. An interactive room equipped with screens delves into the process from creation to the sale of each garment. In Yves Saint Laurent's own words, "I would like my dresses and my drawings to be studied in a hundred years." The museum is now ensuring the enduring legacy of his spectacular collections.

Address 5 avenue Marceau, 75116 Paris, +33 (0)1 44 31 64 00, museeyslparis.com, contact@museeyslparis.com | Getting there Metro to Alma-Marceau (Line 9); bus 42, 63, 72, 80, 92 to Alma-Marceau | Hours Tue & Wed, Fri–Sun 11am–6pm, Thu 11am–9pm | Tip You can continue your introduction to fashion by visiting La Galerie Dior (11 rue François Ier, www.galeriedior.com).

# 111 Zadkine Museum

*The master of direct carving*

It is rare to find artists who would open their studios to the general public. Yet this was the last wish of Ossip Zadkine (1888–1967), a master of direct carving and a major figure in the Paris School avant-garde movement. Enamored with his garden, the sculptor lived in this house with his wife for forty years, unable to imagine living anywhere else but within this direct relationship between art and nature. The Zadkine Museum opened in 1982, thanks to a bequest by the artist's widow Valentine Prax (1897–1981) that included drawings, photos, tapestries, and sculptures.

An expatriate from Belarus, Zadkine moved to Paris in 1910 and studied at Beaux-Arts in Paris, where he'd meet Pablo Picasso, Guillaume Apollinaire, and Amedeo Modigliani. In 1928, he moved into this studio near the Montparnasse district where many immigrant artists were settling, and he lived and worked here until his death. You will see the variety of media used by the sculptor, including wood, stone, marble, and bronze. The collection, dispersed throughout the house, workshop, and garden, comprises several hundred sculptures and an equivalent number of works on paper, such as gouaches, drawings, and documentary photographs. The artwork spans from the primitivism of his early years to cubism, and culminates in the lyrical expressions of his later years.

Zadkine's work is colossal, consisting of immense and striking sculptures that exude strength, force and emotion. But his sculptures are anything but monolithic. In his words, "My objective is to transport and transform the viewer by creating an object that evokes a sense of lightness and movement while creating artwork that has the power to engage and move the human being emotionally." Zadkine's graphic output, a lesser-known feature of his oeuvre, was also immense. Drawing and painting occupied a significant portion of his time, always complementing his sculptural works.

Address 100 bis rue d'Assas, 75006 Paris, +33 (0)1 55 42 77 20, www.zadkine.paris.fr, musee.zadkine@paris.fr | Getting there Metro to Notre-Dame des Champs (Line 12), Vavin (Line 4); RER B to Port-Royal; bus 83 to Michelet, 38, 82 to Val de Grâce, 91 to Campagne Première | Hours Tue–Sun 10am–6pm | Tip Other famous people who lived on Rue Notre-Dame-des-Champs include Victor Hugo (no. 27), the painter Fernand Léger (no. 86), and the painter Othon Friesz (no. 73). The façade of 82 rue Notre-Dame-des-Champs is worth seeing, and right next door is a magnificent Art Deco building (26 rue Vavin).

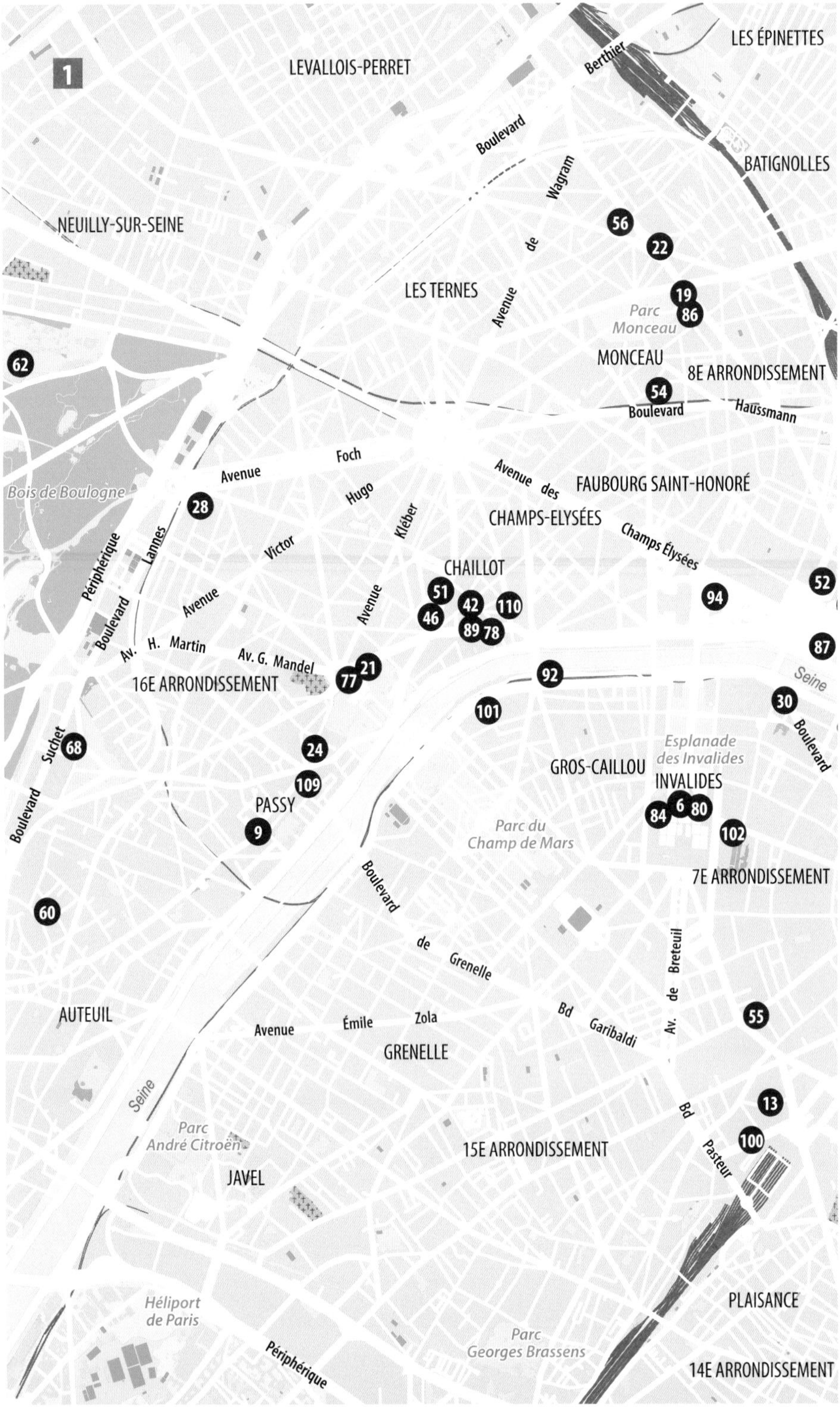
1
LEVALLOIS-PERRET
LES ÉPINETTES
Berthier
Boulevard
BATIGNOLLES
Wagram
de
Avenue
NEUILLY-SUR-SEINE
56
22
LES TERNES
19
86
Parc Monceau
62
MONCEAU
8E ARRONDISSEMENT
54
Boulevard
Haussmann
Avenue
Foch
Avenue des
Champs Élysées
FAUBOURG SAINT-HONORÉ
Bois de Boulogne
28
Hugo
Victor
Avenue
Kléber
CHAMPS-ELYSÉES
Périphérique
Lannes
Boulevard
CHAILLOT
51
42
110
94
52
46
89
78
Avenue
Av. H. Martin
Av. G. Mandel
87
21
77
Seine
16E ARRONDISSEMENT
92
30
101
Boulevard
Esplanade des Invalides
Suchet
68
24
GROS-CAILLOU
INVALIDES
109
PASSY
84
6
80
Boulevard
9
Parc du Champ de Mars
102
7E ARRONDISSEMENT
Boulevard
de
Grenelle
60
Av. de Breteuil
Bd Garibaldi
55
AUTEUIL
Avenue
Émile
Zola
GRENELLE
Seine
13
Bd Pasteur
Parc André Citroën
100
15E ARRONDISSEMENT
JAVEL
PLAISANCE
Héliport de Paris
Parc Georges Brassens
Périphérique
14E ARRONDISSEMENT

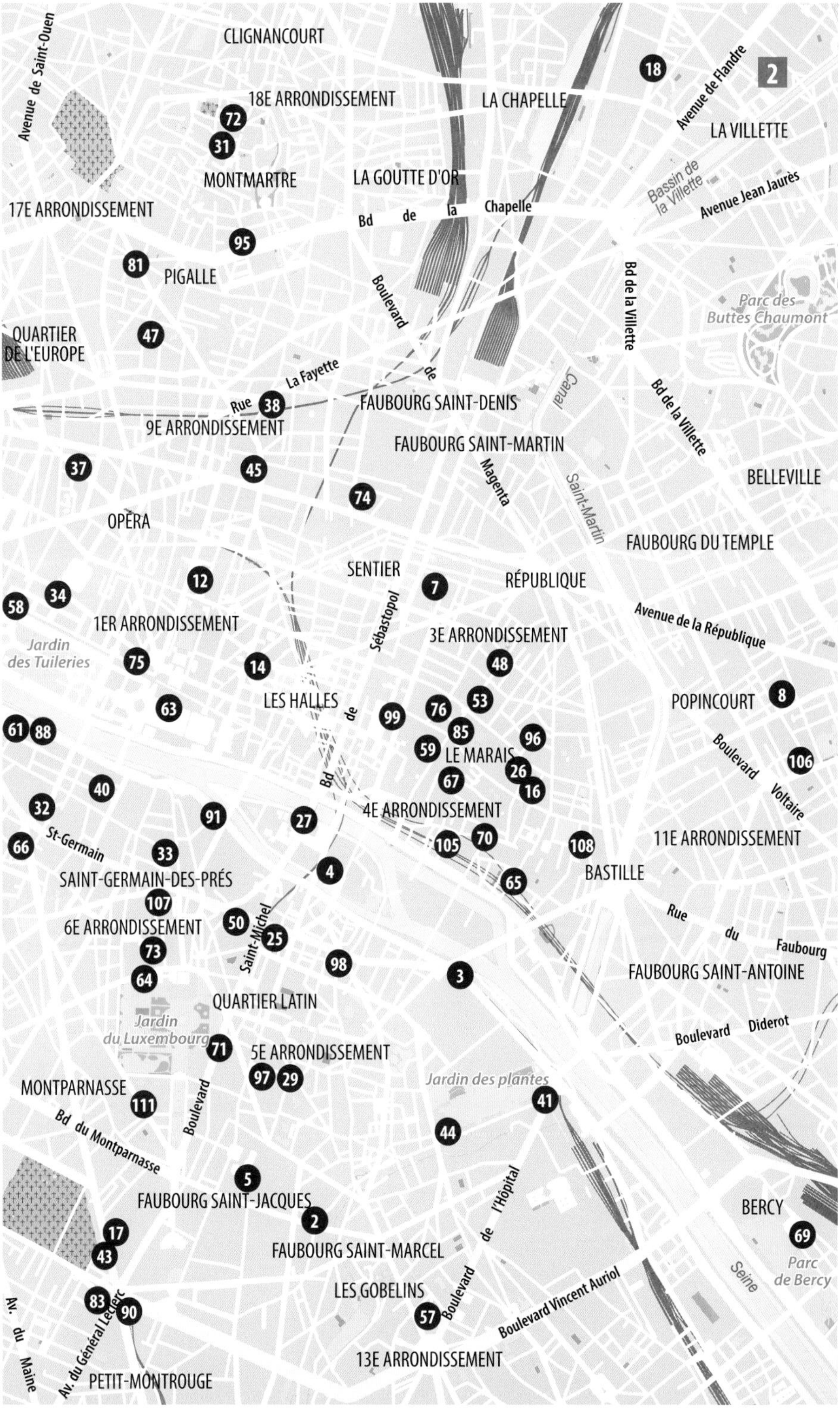
2
CLIGNANCOURT
18E ARRONDISSEMENT
LA CHAPELLE
Avenue de Flandre
LA VILLETTE
Avenue de Saint-Ouen
MONTMARTRE
LA GOUTTE D'OR
17E ARRONDISSEMENT
Bd de la Chapelle
Bassin de la Villette
Avenue Jean Jaurès
PIGALLE
Boulevard de
Bd de la Villette
Parc des Buttes Chaumont
QUARTIER DE L'EUROPE
Rue La Fayette
FAUBOURG SAINT-DENIS
Canal Saint-Martin
9E ARRONDISSEMENT
FAUBOURG SAINT-MARTIN
Magenta
BELLEVILLE
OPÉRA
FAUBOURG DU TEMPLE
SENTIER
RÉPUBLIQUE
Sébastopol
Avenue de la République
1ER ARRONDISSEMENT
3E ARRONDISSEMENT
Jardin des Tuileries
LES HALLES
POPINCOURT
Bd de
LE MARAIS
Boulevard Voltaire
4E ARRONDISSEMENT
St-Germain
11E ARRONDISSEMENT
BASTILLE
SAINT-GERMAIN-DES-PRÉS
6E ARRONDISSEMENT
Saint-Michel
Rue du Faubourg
FAUBOURG SAINT-ANTOINE
QUARTIER LATIN
Jardin du Luxembourg
Boulevard Diderot
5E ARRONDISSEMENT
MONTPARNASSE
Jardin des plantes
Bd du Montparnasse
Boulevard
FAUBOURG SAINT-JACQUES
Boulevard de l'Hôpital
BERCY
FAUBOURG SAINT-MARCEL
Parc de Bercy
Seine
LES GOBELINS
Boulevard Vincent Auriol
Av. du Maine
Av. du Général Leclerc
13E ARRONDISSEMENT
PETIT-MONTROUGE
18
72
31
95
81
47
38
37
45
74
12
7
34
58
75
14
48
53
63
99
76
85
96
8
61
88
59
26
106
40
67
16
32
91
27
105
70
108
66
33
4
65
107
50
25
73
98
3
64
71
97
29
111
41
44
5
2
17
43
69
83
90
57

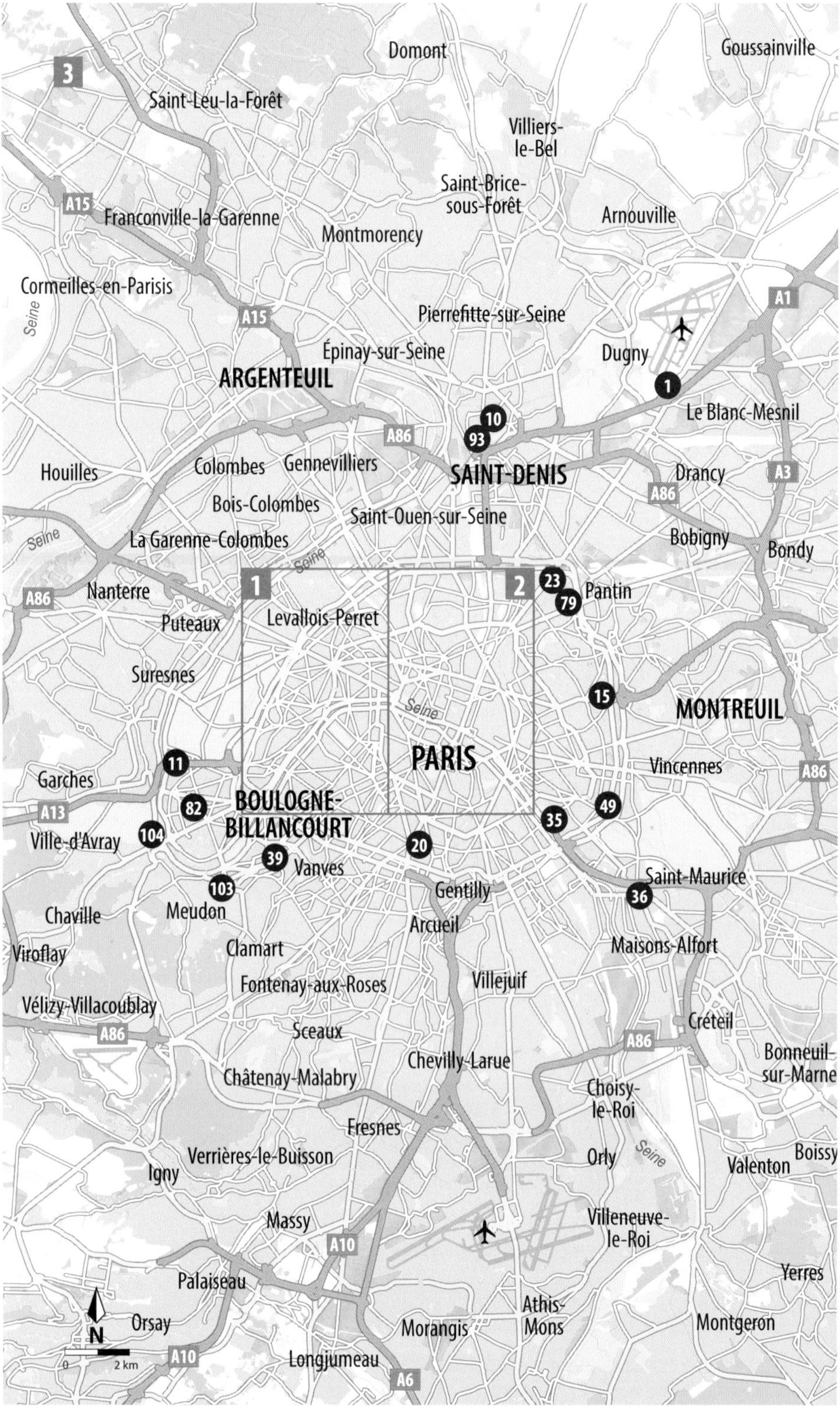

3
Domont
Goussainville
Saint-Leu-la-Forêt
Villiers-
le-Bel
Saint-Brice-
sous-Forêt
A15
Franconville-la-Garenne
Montmorency
Arnouville
Cormeilles-en-Parisis
Seine
A15
Pierrefitte-sur-Seine
A1
Épinay-sur-Seine
Dugny
ARGENTEUIL
1
10
Le Blanc-Mesnil
93
A86
Houilles
Colombes
Gennevilliers
SAINT-DENIS
Drancy
A3
A86
Bois-Colombes
Saint-Ouen-sur-Seine
Seine
La Garenne-Colombes
Bobigny
Bondy
Seine
1
2
23
Pantin
79
A86
Nanterre
Levallois-Perret
Puteaux
Suresnes
15
Seine
MONTREUIL
PARIS
11
Vincennes
A86
Garches
BOULOGNE-
BILLANCOURT
82
49
A13
35
104
Ville-d'Avray
20
39
Vanves
Saint-Maurice
103
Gentilly
36
Chaville
Meudon
Arcueil
Viroflay
Clamart
Maisons-Alfort
Fontenay-aux-Roses
Villejuif
Vélizy-Villacoublay
A86
Sceaux
Créteil
A86
Chevilly-Larue
Bonneuil-
sur-Marne
Châtenay-Malabry
Choisy-
le-Roi
Fresnes
Seine
Boissy
Verrières-le-Buisson
Orly
Valenton
Igny
Massy
Villeneuve-
le-Roi
A10
Palaiseau
Yerres
Athis-
Mons
N
Orsay
Morangis
Montgeron
0
2 km
A10
Longjumeau
A6

Sybil Canac, Renée Grimaud, Katia Thomas
**111 Places in Paris That You Shouldn't Miss**
ISBN 978-3-7408-0159-5

Irène Lassus-Fuchs, Julian Spalding
**111 Tastes of Paris That You Shouldn't Miss**
ISBN 978-3-7408-0581-4

Wendy Lubovich, Ed Lefkowicz
**111 Museums in New York That You Must Not Miss**
ISBN 978-3-7408-0379-7

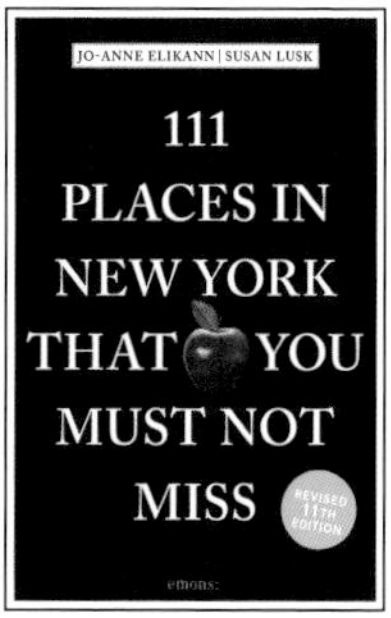


Jo-Anne Elikann, Susan Lusk
**111 Places in New York That You Must Not Miss**
ISBN 978-3-7408-2057-2

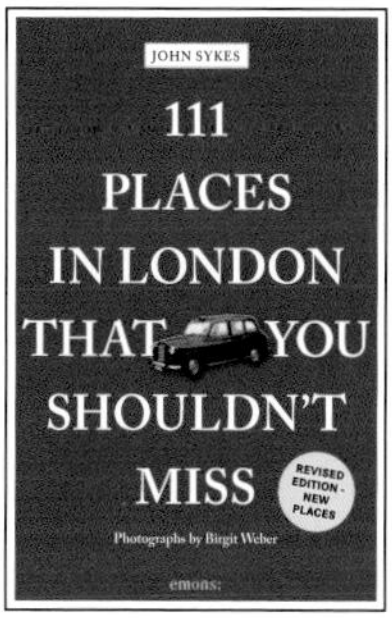


John Sykes, Birgit Weber
**111 Places in London That You Shouldn't Miss**
ISBN 978-3-7408-1644-5

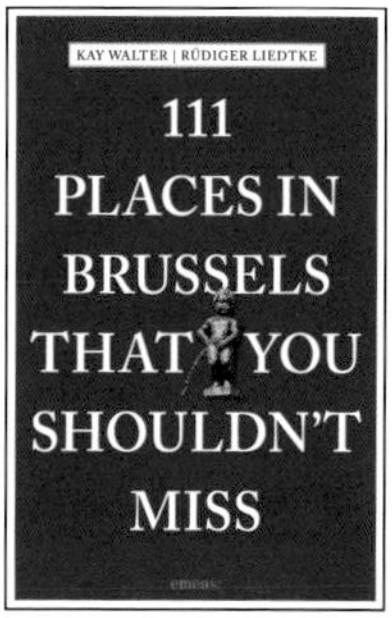


Kay Walter, Rüdiger Liedtke
**111 Places in Brussels That You Shouldn't Miss**
ISBN 978-3-7408-0259-2

Thomas Fuchs
**111 Places in Amsterdam That You Shouldn't Miss**
ISBN 978-3-7408-0023-9

Rüdiger Liedtke
**111 Places in Mallorca That You Shouldn't Miss**
ISBN 978-3-7408-1049-8

Catrin Ponciano
**111 Places along the Algarve That You Shouldn't Miss**
ISBN 978-3-7408-0381-0

**Photo Credits**

Bourdelle Museum (ch. 13): © 2022 Pierre Antoine Studio;

Bourse de Commerce-Pinault Collection (ch. 14): Photo by Patrick Tourneboeuf;

Cartier Foundation (ch. 17): Photo by Thibaut Voisin, 2022;

Chana Orloff Atelier-Museum (ch. 20): © Stephane Briolant;

Gallery of Paleontology & Comparative Anatomy (ch. 41): © MNHN – Betrand Faye;

Giacometti Institute (ch. 43): Photo courtesy of the Fondation-Giacometti-Institut;

Grand Gallery of Evolution (ch. 44): © MNHN – Jean-Christophe Domenech;

Guimet Museum (ch. 46): © Musée national des arts asiatiques – Guimet, Paris / Photo Vincent Leroux, 2021;

Henri Cartier-Bresson Foundation (ch. 48): Accueil de la Fondation HCB, 79 rue des Archives, novembre 2018 © Cyrille Weiner;

Hotêl d'Heidelbach (ch. 52): © Musée national des arts asiatiques – Guimet, Paris / Photo Vincent Leroux, 2021;

Jean Dubuffet Foundation (ch. 55): Façade of the Jean Dubuffet Foundation, © Fondation Dubuffet, Paris;

Lafayette Anticipations (ch. 59): © Marc Domage, Lafayette Anticipations;

Le Corbusier Foundation (ch. 60): Olivier Martin Gambier © Fondation Le Corbusier;

Museum of the Liberation of Paris (ch. 83): © Pierre Antoine / Paris Musées / Musée de la Liberation de Paris – Musée du Général Leclerc – Musée Jean Moulin;

Quai Branly – Jacques Chirac Museum (ch. 101): © musée du quai Branly-Jacques Chirac, the Main Collections Level, (top) photo by Thomas Garnier, (bottom) photo by Vincent Mercier;

Yves Saint Laurent Museum (ch. 110): © Luc Castel;

Zadkine Museum (ch. 111): Garden and façade of the musée Zadkine, Paris photographie © Pierre Antoine Studio

**Art Credits**

Atelier des Lumières (ch. 8): *L'Eglise d'auvers-sur-Oise* (1890) by Vincent van Gogh;

Bourdelle Museum (ch. 13): Interior garden overlooking the façades of the studio spaces, Bourdelle Museum, Paris;

Cartier Foundation (ch. 17): *Mirdidingkingathi Juwarnda Sally Gabori Exhibition*, Fondation Cartier pour l'art contemporain, Paris, 2022 © VG Bild-Kunst, Bonn 2023;

Chana Orloff Atelier-Museum (ch. 20): Sculptures by Chana Orloff © VG Bild-Kunst, Bonn 2023;

Dalí Paris (ch. 31): *Éléphant de Triomphe* (1975) by Salvador Dalí © Salvador Dalí, Fundació Gala-Salvador Dalí/VG Bild-Kunst, Bonn 2023;

Eugène Delacroix Museum (ch. 33): Paintings by Eugène Delacroix, courtesy of The Eugène Delacroix National Museum and the Louvre Museum;

Gustave Moreau National Museum (ch. 47): Paintings by Gustave Moreau;

Hunting & Nature Museum (ch. 53): *Saint Eustace* by Lucas Cranach;

Jean-Jacques Henner National Museum (ch. 56): Paintings by Jean-Jacques Henner;

Maillol Museum (ch. 66): Sculptures by Aristide Maillol;

Marmottan Monet Museum (68): Paintings by Berthe Morisot, from left to right, *Fillette au jersey bleu* (1886), *Julie Manet et sa levrette Laërte* (1893), *Les Foins à Bougival* (1883), *Eugene Manet et sa fille dans le jardin de Bougival* or *À la campagne* (1881), *Le Cerisier* (1891);

Museum of Decorative Arts (ch. 75): Furniture by Hector Guimard, courtesy of the Museum of Decorative Arts;

Museum of Modern Art (ch. 78): From left to right, *Rythme* (1938) by Sonia Delaunay; *Rythme no 2* (1938) by Robert Delaunay, *Floating Woman* (1927) by Gaston Lachaise;

Nissim de Camondo Museum (ch. 86) Courtesy of the musée Nissim de Camondo;

Petit Palais (ch. 94): *L'approvisionnement des Halles* (1891) by Léon Augustin Lhermitte; sculptures, from left to right, *La porteuse de pain* by Jules Félix Coutan (1882), *La Pêche* by Alexandre Falguière (1880-1883), *La Moisson* by Henri Chapu (1883);

Quai Branly-Jacques Chirac Museum (ch. 101): The Main Collections Level, (top) Details from the Oceania Zone, (bottom) Overview of the Oceania Zone, © musée du quai Branly-Jacques Chirac;

Rodin Museum (ch. 102): Sculptures by Auguste Rodin;

Rodin Museum Meudon (ch. 103): *Les Bourgeois de Calais* (1889) by Auguste Rodin;

Sèvres Museum (ch. 104): *Vase de Neptune* (1867), Manufacture de Sèvres;

Trade Guild Museum (ch. 107): Museum attached to the Fédération des Compagnons du Tour de France Ile de France, 2 Rue de Guermantes, 77400 Saint-Thibault-des-Vignes

I would like to express my deepest gratitude to James Wesolowski, my fun and ever supportive co-author. Thanks to my editor Karen Seiger and for giving me the incredible opportunity to work on this project. The experience allowed me to pursue my passion, and sharing all these unexpected discoveries together has been an absolute joy. I want to thank my daughters Olivia and Julianne, whose curiosity and joy for life have infused my writing with a sense of enthusiasm and wonder for which I am forever grateful.
Many thanks to the curators, guides, and staff members at the museums for their extensive knowledge and for taking the time to answer all my endless questions. They shared thoughtful stories and insights that allowed me to consider their collections with a fresh perspective. Their dedication and passion are a precious contribution to the preservation and dissemination of French cultural heritage.
*Anne Carminati*

All my love to my brilliant wife Karen, who enthusiastically supports all my endeavors and who makes every day the best day of my life. My undying gratitude to my wonderful co-author Anne Carminati, who so kindly agreed to work with me on this project and then happily covered most of the serious fine art institutions so that I could indulge my love of history as well as unique and unusual museums. A warm embrace to my dear friends and fellow museum lovers Michèle Marchadier and Yves Demars, with whom Karen and I have visited so many special places in France over the past 15 years. My thanks to all the museums that agreed to participate in this guide and to the many gracious and welcoming people who have been so generous with their time and expertise. Together, you have created an incredible collection of museums in a singularly spectacular city.
*James Wesolowski*

**Anne Carminati** is a free spirit. Free of boundaries and bias, eager to listen, to discover, and to create. A native Parisian, Anne's greatest passions are art and design. She attended art schools in both Paris and New York. Now, she works as an interior designer for Maison Anne Carminati based in Paris and New York, recently launching a new high-end home accessories website. Anne's taste combines a love of historic traditions and cultures with emerging art trends to bring energy, creativity, and new perspectives.

**James Wesolowski** fell in love with Paris when he first visited as a young man. After university, he lived and worked throughout the world and then settled in New York City, where he runs a technology consulting firm. James splits his time between New York and Paris, where he pursues interests in museums, French wine and cuisine, photography, and running marathons. His fantasy is to study art restoration and work on paintings in one of Paris' many small churches.